To Your Best Health

Fifth Edition

Magnetic Therapy
FACTS

Ancient Medicine

to

Space Age
Technology

Dr. George McDermott

Scott & McDermott Publishing

Scott & McDermott Publishing, 2700 N.W. 1st Terrace, Pompano Beach, FL 33064

The information contained herein is obtained from sources believed to be reliable, but its accuracy cannot be guaranteed.

Library of Congress Cataloging-in-Publication Data
McDermott, George
Magnetic Therapy Facts
Includes bibliographical references (p.) and index
1. Magnetic Therapy 2. Health 3. Natural Science 4. Longevity

Magnetic Therapy Facts
ISBN 0-9667384-8-9

Published in the USA

All material in this publication is provided for information only and may not be construed as medical advice or instruction. No action or inaction should be taken based solely on the contents of this publication; instead, readers should consult appropriate health professionals on any matter relating to their health and well-being. The information and opinions provided in this publication are believed to be accurate and sound, based on the best judgment available to the author, but readers who fail to consult with appropriate health authorities assume risk or any injuries. The publisher is not responsible for errors or omissions.

Dedicated to:

Gus Lovett
and
Rick Perkins

Who have devoted their
careers to the advancement
of magnetic therapy and
to the thousands who have
received beneficial health
results

Contents

Forward

Magnetic forces helps heal more ailments at lower cost than any other treatment modality except possibly chicken soup, mother's love and aspirin. Magnetic forces, in my experience, seem to work on about 80% of the common ailments, 80% of the time.

Magnetism is a universal force, like gravity, which shapes the structure of our lives at every level from electrons to atoms, molecules, cells, organs, and glands. Biophysics, biochemistry, cell and organ functioning, blood flow, enzyme activity, brain wave activity and glandular activity are all affected by extremely small magnetic forces. Moreover, we live in the magnetic nest of the whole Earth which is called the geomagnetic field. This field in turn varies slightly, but significantly, for our sensitive organisms, with the position of the Moon, the planets, the activity of the Sun, and probably influences from other stars and galaxies, even though we have not the instruments to measure such effects. Magnetic forces, in their infinite variations guide our form and functioning at every level. They influence our health for the better and for the worst from minor aches and pains to major ailments, mental disturbances, and even such a mass condition as international wars, a kind of mass psychosis which correlates with solar magnetic activity changes every eleven years as sunspot numbers rise, and two or three years later as they fall.

Natural Magnetic therapy has been known and used for thousands of years by savvy healers who could use only weak natural magnetic rocks and powders found on the surface of the Earth. With the discovery of electricity and metal working technology, silent, non-invasive, magnetic forces are now being focused, organized, and controlled by humans to help heal diseases of all kinds. Dr. George McDermott has carefully researched major ailments and their treatment with magnetic therapy. In many cases the results are minor miracles; especially for the patient, who may have had some irritating or debilitating condition for years.

This book is a must for a health library. It is a miniature encyclopedia of major ailments and their treatments.

How do magnetic forces work?

At the smallest level, magnetic forces act on the hydrogen protons which are very much smaller than the molecules which drugs work on. So this is probably why magnetic forces work on a larger variety than drugs which mostly work on the molecular level. Protons, when stimulated by magnetic forces tilt a bit in their mad dance and give out little squeals of delight or alarm depending on the nature of the impinging magnetic forces. Cell phone microwaves, geomagnetic storms, all frequencies of light and radio waves and sound waves can interfere with our biochemistry as well as physical, emotional and mental trauma. Although they are emitted as radio waves they can turn into sound waves. These inaudible (to us) sounds and radio waves help hydrogen atoms bond to one another and to other atoms. Much of the workings of the body depend on hydrogen bonding chemistry. Dr. McDermott describes many other mechanisms in this comprehensive book. Your body probably will love the calming magnetic force from a magnetic bed which is steady and even, not chaotic. However, no books read can really tell you if a bed will work, or how well or quickly it will work for your health needs if you have any. You must get a bed and try it for your own health.

Editor's note:

Buryl Payne, holds Ph.D. in psychology and an M.S. in physics. He has been doing magnetic therapy for over twenty years. He has written several magnetic therapy books, designed electronic magnetic field generators and discovered a way to measure a form of subtle magnetism which also may be part of magnetic therapy treatments. He lives in Santa Cruz, CA and is an avid surfer and outdoorsman.

Magnetic Therapy

"Humanity never learns anything from the "nay" sayers.
It is up to you to try new ways to find out what is best for you.
Listen to your own conscious, not your neighbors."
Thomas Edison

The use of magnets as a therapy is not new and records show their use by ancient Hindu teachings in "The Vedas" in 2000 BC. The ancient Egyptians and Greeks mention magnets as a form of healing as long ago as 300 BC and are mentioned in records written by Aristotle and Pliny.

Ann Gill Taylor, R.N., from the University of Virginia, says, "We did find a statistically significant difference in pain intensity reduction for one of the active magnet pad groups. The two groups that slept on pads with active magnets generally showed the greatest improvements in outcome scores of pain intensity level, number of tender points on the body and functional status after 6 months.

The science and use of magnetic navigation and healing has been practiced by ancient Chinese, Persians, and Vikings. Because many Americans have been fed up with the ever burdening cost of medical care and its sometimes failures, it has forced them to look for alternative therapies for their aches and pains. A host of therapies have surfaced some old, some new; Chiropractic, massage, acupuncture, herbal, vitamins, biofeedback, homeopathy, and permanent magnets are just a few therapies offered. Magnetic therapy has the most appeal, because of its effectiveness. It is a natural therapy, non toxic, no pills, no needles, no salves, no side effects and most important, a one time low cost for everyone. Magnetic therapy, when coupled with professional medicial treatments, proper nutrition and exercise, has proven to be the most effective and economical in healping people with a host of problems.

Biomagnetism works in the human body through the circulatory system, the nervous system and the endocrine system. Magnetism is continually penetrating every known particle, right down to the single cell. Its ordering effect on living systems arise from the fact that magnetism is a blueprint of life itself. All known energies have, as a base, this electromagnetic field. The latest research indicates that magnetism has a very significant, beneficial, biological effect on human beings.

Blood contains ferrous hemoglobin (iron) that functions as a carrier of oxygen and carbon dioxide. As blood circulates through the lungs, fully magnetized ferrous hemoglobin is able to transport more oxygen to cell tissues as well as taking more carbon dioxide waste from the cell back to the lungs for removal. This means more energy and less fatigue as tissue cells and internal organs stay substantially healthier. Many people report an energy reserve allowing them to fully face each day with greater concentration and much less fatigue. Magnetic pillows, shoe insoles, and seat cushions continue to recharge the body's magnetism for a full day's cycle of 24 hours. The human body, like the earth, is a biomagnetic unit that vibrates at approximately 7.9 cycles per second of direct current.

It is amazing, yet it is also common sense, that your body electro-magnetically vibrates at the same frequency as the earth. When we tire, our body rhythm slows down in relationship to the earth. When we are out of sync with Mother Earth, it is then that fatigue, illness and disease have the best opportunity to overtake our health. By use of supplemental magnetic therapy devices, we are able to assist and boost our vibrational energy levels back up to our natural balance.

Dr. Nakagawa, of Isuzu Hospital in Tokyo, Japan, has identified a malady that he calls "Magnetic Deficiency Syndrome." It is believed that we call this problem Chronic Fatigue Syndrome.

Magnets are used in spacecraft to protect the astronauts from bone loss, disorientation, and other magnetic deficiencies. Magnetic Therapy is the cutting edge of a healing, healthy energy boom that is sure to revolutionize the way we treat our bodies.

Studies on magnetic therapies in the *Journal of Electro-and Magnetobiology* led some pioneering doctors in this country to experiment with magnets in their practice. Their activities helped to standardize the use of some magnets, the magnet size and strength in treating various conditions. The length of exposure to a magnet for healing certain ailments was also determined. Because of their work we know which magnets work most efficiently; for example, a magnet

James Souder
Norso Biomagnetics
Studies performed on animals, and microscopic examination of blood vessels, indicate that capillary blood flow is stimulated by the movement of magnetic fields through tissue and is the dominant factor in magnetic field therapy.

3

placed in one specific area of the body may not activate the entire body's healing power, whereas sleeping on a magnetic bed pad radiates a magnetic field that can penetrate evenly into every part of the body and boost the entire immune system.

Magnetic energy has different names. Some people call it *energy* or *life force*; the Chinese call it *Chi*, the Indians know it as *Prana*. Whatever you choose to call it, magnetic energy is one of Enstein's four forces of the Universe. (radiation, nuclear, gravity, and magnetic) It pulses throughout the galaxies and is found everywhere in nature.

Science knows that the human body is composed of numerous cells that combine to form blood, tissues, bones and organs. These cells are in the constant state of renewing themselves. Dr. Robert Becker, one of the leading medical doctors who advocates the use of magnets in healing, believes that the force which stimulates cellular growth and division is electromagnetic energy.

He and other scientists contend that the charge on the cells of the body becomes depleted as cells perform their normal daily functions and that the body tries to "recharge" the worn down cells by sending pulses of electromagnetic energy from the brain through the nervous system.

While there are many applications claimed for magnetics from the reduction of scar tissue to the treatment of internal organs, the predominant use of magnetic devices is the treatment of musculoskeletal pain.

There is a consensus that heightened blood flow to the area under the footprint of the magnet is one of the primary results of magnetic treatment. The results have been demonstrated by both thermographic and nuclear medicine studies. There has also been evidence of pain blocking phenomena in certain nerve fibers related to the application of magnetic fields. Researchers have been able to demonstrate changes in the electrical potential of nerve cells that magnetic therapy lowers the threshold for transmitting pain impulses from the pain site to the receptors in the brain.

Dr. Dean Bonlie, Chairman of the Scientific Committee of the North American Academy of Magnetic Therapy, explains that when the body is fatigued, a "loss of static charge" on the body's cells causes a "clumping of red blood cells." Through magnetic field supplementation, he says, chemical reactions are enhanced, building up the charge on cell walls which cause the cells to repel each other, reducing the clumping. With more surface area available, he says, the oxygen-carrying capacity of the cells is increased which in turn reinvigorates the body.

While the physics of magnetic energy is debated, its benefits are being experienced by people around the country. Dr. Ronald Lawrence of Agoura Hills, California asserts that magnets have been extremely effective in the control of arthritic pain in many of his patients. Dee Massengale, an exercise physiologist in Atlanta, Georgia suffering with fibromyaglia since 1982, says that of all the therapies she's tried magnetic therapy has been one of the most valuable tools for pain management.

In one of our own experiments, Anne Ziseiman of Hollywood, Florida slept with magnet wraps strapped above her knee cap. She reported a reduction of arthritic swelling and a softening of the inflammation after four nights of use.

Magnetic fields work much more quickly and effectively than heat, infrared light, anti-inflammatory drugs, trigger-point injections or microwave diathermy. It's likely to be four or six months before an injured skier or other athlete is back in play again from the conventional treatment of ice, followed by heat to reduce swelling. Heat alone will not stimulate therapeutic repair of injured tissue or muscle. An ample supply of nutrient-rich blood is needed. Healing requires resumption of normal blood flow to the injured site, not simply pain relief. In magnetic therapy, knee braces can be removed more quickly; weightlifters can reduce lower back pain, sciatica (inflammation of sciatic nerve running down the hip and thigh) and carpal tunnel syndrome can be relieved.

Osteopathic physician Sanford Paul, Mercerville, NJ, is convinced of the effectiveness of magnetic therapy. "Though I use conventional medical methods, I find that the application of biomagnets has helped in some difficult traumatic-injury cases. I feel that biomagnets should be part of the total armamentarium of future physicians," he says.

Orthopedic chiropractor Kurt Vreeland, White

River Junction, Vermont, physician for the U.S. Olympic ski jumping team, uses magnets for ski and other injuries. "I have used magnets with good results on everything from rotator cuff injuries to what they used to call in football "hip-pointer."

If you are thinking about purchasing magnetic therapy for yourself, or loved ones, you are making a wise choice which has been proven effective for centuries. If you have already bought a magnetic device, like a sleep system, insoles or seat cushion, you are to be commended for your intelligent decision. Remembering what Dr. Albert Einstein said about naysayers, who are often jealous or uninformed, it is up to you to make up your mind for what is best for you and your family. Rest assure, magnetic therapy is the right decision.

History of Magnets

*"The only thing holding humanity back is the fear of
something new or which they do not understand. In order to
benefit ourselves we must try new things."*
— *Albert Einstein*

Magnetism is one of the original forces that created the Universe. The human inquiring mind is always
uncovering the vast mysteries of this ever present power
and the silent, complex control it has over our daily
lives. This book is written for the person interested in the
general healing aspects of magnets and not the in-depth
scientific explanation of how magnets do the things they
do. So we will dispense with the science and focus on
how magnets can help you with your medical problems
now and keep you healthy in the future.

Magnetism is basically aligning the atoms of an
element so that they are in a line with the positive end
touching the negative end. Picture a circus when the
elephants come marching in with each elephant's trunk
holding on to the tail in front. This is magnetism.

SUMMARY
Magnets and magnetism have been with us since
the world began. This chapter gives a short history
of this universal force and how we often take it for
granted in our daily lives.

Magnetism is everywhere. No matter how small, all
objects have a positive and negative pole because every
thing is composed of atoms. A simple piece of string has

two poles. If you cut the string in two, you now have four poles, and each subsequent cut piece of string down to the tiniest will have two poles. Also, within a large object, you can have continually smaller, opposite poles all the way down to individual atoms where it stops.

For example, within our solar system the sun is a positive pole and all the revolving planets are negative poles.

Impossible.... Maybe?

In the beginning of the 20th century, as physicists mapped the atomic construction, an eerie realization emerged. The atom fluorine and the Solar System have an awkward resemblance. Both have a magnetic positive center (sun/proton) with nine negative satellites (planets/electrons) circumnavigating. What if, our solar system was but an atom in an immensely larger dimension? No one can rule out the possibility.

Now the Sun itself has an internal negative and positive poles. Earth too, is a negative pole to the Sun, but we also have a north and south pole internally. It is important for you to understand that magnetic fields can coexist in a large body and then in consecutively smaller and smaller fields within these large bodies. Just like those famous Russian dolls, when you open one there is another inside, and when you open that doll, there is another. Magnetic fields can be scaled down within smaller and smaller fields until they get to the end of the line which is always the individual atom.

Magnetic forces are universal. They are found everywhere and are quietly involved in almost every physical event that effects humans. Everything from the orbits of galaxies, solar systems and planets down to the heavenly revolutions of comets, moons and man-made satellites, all are calmly moved by the ever present force of magnetism.

The electro-magnetic wave lengths dominate our world. These invisible waves of energy which pulsate from the low frequency radio waves to high frequency gamma x-rays are everywhere in our world. The visible band of electro-magnetic waves enable us to see, without them we would be blind. Without them we would receive no sunlight to grow food nor infrared or microwaves to cook our food, and it certainly would be a quiet world without radio or television transmissions.

Not only does magnetic forces control the heavens above and the ground below, but this power goes down to the elementary atoms which comprise every single thing, both organic and inorganic because it controls the spin of the electrons as they circle the nucleus of every atom. It is impossible to either underestimate or overestimate this invisible force of magnetism in our daily lives because it so quietly controls everything we do.

North Pole Paradise
Earth's poles are constantly moving inches every year. Eons ago the North Pole was around Hawaii, and its present location was a warm swamp. Proof is Spitsbergen, an island covered by the northern polar cap, and Alaska's north shore, both have huge oil and coal deposits left when the area was hot and steamy.

The word magnet is derived from ancient Greek people "the Magnetes" who hail from the province Magnesia which is just north of Athens, Greece. There lying on the ground were natural, magnetic lodestones, the common product of local, ancient volcanic eruptions. From magnesia we not only got the word magnets, but also magnesium (a mineral), Milk of Magnesia (a laxative) and according to folk lore, the word magic because the Magnetes by using magnets became the first magicians through the magical attraction of magnets. According to the tales of Homer, these people would sew magnets into the lining of their pants. They would set up a small table in the marketplace and produce puppet shows. The base of the toy figurines would have magnets in them and by manipulating their knees under the table (unseen by the crowd) the little puppets would magically move without strings or by touch. Upon inspection, the onlookers could never understand how the puppets moved across the tabletop...except by "magic" from the man from Magnesia.

Most people are introduced to the magical power of magnets as children for they are incorporated into many little children's toys because they are fascinating, yet very safe to play with. You can keep a five-year old child amused for hours by simply giving them a pair of magnets and some paper clips. They will immediately notice the magnetic attraction when the opposite poles draw together and when like poles repel each other. They will build little trains from the steel paper clips (the stronger the magnet, the longer the train) and will laugh with delight as they test your home appliances for steel made products. They many even notice that the paper clips become little magnets after brief exposure to the magnets.

Magnets are excellent teaching tools because they get the child to ask questions about science and the nature of the things around them. All you need are some small ten gauss refrigerator magnets, a five year old child and you will soon see the wonders of experimentation and the wonders of the educational process. Questions will soon arise from this young, questioning mind. What is this supernatural force that moves things, but I can't see, touch, taste, smell or hear it? Why does a magnet stick to one thing and not to another? How come one side sticks to one magnet, and the other side pushes it away? Can you explain why one magnet will move another magnet through wood, glass or plastic, but I can't feel a thing? Aren't magnets wonderful?

The use of magnets has even entered into our speech patterns. We often talk about a particularly dynamic person as having a "magnetic personality" because this individual has the personal magnetism to attract many people. The Rev. Billy Graham, Martin Luther King and President John F. Kennedy all had a positive, personal magnetism. On the other pole, we could say that Adolph Hitler, Chairman Mao and Rev. Jimmy Jones who attracted all the religious people in Guyana, led millions to their deaths through their negative magnetic attraction. Another phrase often used in common English usage is that "opposites attract" which refers to the opposite North-South poles coming together. Recent scientific research into genetics, pheromones are evidence that our own bodies are highly magnetized.

Hippocrates, the father of medicine, promoted the use of magnets for pain relief, fracture repair and of course to get arrowheads out of the muscles of wounded soldiers. In 2000 B.C., the healing powers of magnets spread throughout the Mediterranean basin. The Romans would magnetize their shields because they would attract arrows and swords rather than to themselves. The Phoenicians magnetized their oarlocks and a girdle on their oars to keep them in place better during rowing. Queen

Cleopatra of Egypt used magnetic jewelry to preserve her natural beauty and the Vikings would put magnets in their boots and wear magnetic belts for increased vigor.

Switching Poles

This last January, 2001, the Sun's magnetic poles switched. This event happens every 11 years, accompanied by massive solar flares and static interference here on Earth. Our poles also switch about once every 50,000 years. As our natural, ground level gauss rating keeps diminishing (it is now down to 0.5 gauss, in Biblical times it was 2.0 gauss) we are nearing the magnetic switch. No one knows how catastrophic this event it will be, but everything electrical will be affected as the global polarities change. It could happen tomorrow or 5,000 years from now, we have no way of knowing other than it has happened many times before.

The Chinese used magnets as compasses to become the greatest seafarers of the ancient world in 1000 B.C. It was always assumed that American Indians of Chinese stock came across the Siberian-Alaskan land bridge by foot, but new evidence shows that they also used boats to sail down the coast. Chinese writing has been found in Central America and through DNA research it is now proven conclusively that the Polynesians of Hawaii were genetically linked to Chinese. It is only through the use of the magnetic compass that the thousands of miles of Pacific open ocean could have been traversed.

The ancient Chinese had the healing concept of Qi (also known as chi), which is considered your life force as it flows through the meridians of your body and is the basis for acupuncture. Magnets as well as needles can help stimulate this life force to bring a sick, unbalanced body back to health. Many modern American physicians who prefer to use invasive surgery and risky drugs to heal their patients often scoff at these ancient remedies that have been practiced for centuries in China, India and the Mediterranean countries of Ancient Greece, Egypt, Israel and Italy. However, these old Holistic practices had much success in balancing the body and restoring health through methods not understood by modern medicine.

The Chinese healers used their hands and the natural magnetic energy generated within some naturally gifted Qi Gong healers to bring to balance the yin (negative polarity) and the yang (positive polarity) that stop the blockage of your natural energy. In the Egyptian pyramids archeologists have found magnets buried with the pharaohs and hieroglyphics on the walls portraying the use of magnets in healing ceremonies. In the American Indian culture, magnets were often used to heal wounded warriors. The Mesabi Range in northern Minnesota and the Mogollon Range near Sedona, Arizona have long been considered the American Indian's "happy hunting grounds" where they would go to be healed and/or die. Recent scientific research has measured the gauss ratings of these two natural healing locations and the readings have been astronomical compared to the surrounding areas. This is also true of Lourdes, France where the shrine to St. Bernadette has recorded thousands of miraculous healings over hundreds of years has now been found to possess a remarkably high degree of magnetic energy.

Where did all these ancient people get the magnets? Natural magnets are found throughout the world lying on the ground. They are the result of volcanic eruptions. When the lava pours forth from a volcano it solidifies from its molten iron base and breaks into lodestones which have been magnetized from the stress, friction and pressure of the volcano. The Greeks and Romans called them magnets,the Chinese called them tzhu shih (lovingstones because they hugged each other) and the English, Germans and Vikings called them lad (which means the "way" because they used them as compasses). Eventually, they became known as a lodestone (guiding stone) just like the Polaris (North star) became known as the lodestar (guiding star) to these Northern European sailors on their way to the New World of America.

Our modern world would not be possible without the silent aid of magnets. Magnets are at the core of every electrical plant. The heart of every dynamo, turbo and generator ever used to produce electricity has a magnet. When you turn on a light, feel the coolness of your air conditioning or watch television remember a magnet is in there somewhere making it all possible. When you start your car there is a magnetic coil converting the 12 volts from your battery to the 20,000 volts for your spark plug; otherwise, you'll just sit there.

Magnets are all around our homes. Magnetic latches close our kitchen cabinets, decorate our refrigerator doors and pick up pins around the sewing machine. Magnets are partly responsible for the function of our doorbell, radio, television, computers, telephone and microwave oven. Without magnetism none of these appliances could work. Magnetic audio, video tape, and computer discs all store information by use of magnetism. It would be a pretty quiet world without the ever present magnet.
In an industrial world without magnets there would be no electrical generation for production, fabrication or transportation. Large electromagnets pick up whole cars in

15

junkyards, and I once saw a railroad crane pick up a train car and put it back on the tracks. The future of railroads lie in the new magnetic levitation technology which raises the whole train a gentle 4" above the guideway and the new Japanese MAGLEV experimental train set a world rail speed record of 321mph. The operational expenses are much cheaper and a totally clean operation with no pollutants, smoke or noise. Eventually, scientists hope to bring the MAGLEV technology to the automobiles of the future to eliminate the smog from our cities and the greenhouse gases which cause global warming.

A Sign of Magnetic Attraction

In the field of medicine, magnets play a vital role in medical diagnostic procedures (Chapter IV will be about magnetic therapy in medicine). Magnets enable our doctors to check out heartbeats through electro-cardiograms (EKG) which makes a graph of our heart functions, pulsating lines show the doctor how healthy our hearts are. The electroencephalograph (EEG) also shows brain waves so that a neurosurgeon or physiatrist can judge the physical or mental health of the patient. The greatest diagnostic device is the MRI (magnetic resonance imaging). The X-ray, invented in 1895, was a breakthrough so we could finally look through the skin into fractured bones and bad teeth. However, the X-ray gives off deadly radiation which killed many, including one of the founders, Dr. Marie Curie, who was unaware of the deadly radiation. In 1977, the first MRI's became operational. Since magnetism emits no radiation they are perfectly safe to use without the need for protective devices used in X-ray technology. MRI is also much more sensitive than X-rays, gives a better, clearer picture and can also detect soft tissue so it can be used to detect blood flow, cardiovascular problems and cancerous tumors not picked up by X-rays. MRI technology has saved countless thousands of lives through the miracle of magnets.

Since 1903, every U.S. Navy ship passes seawater through a magnetic field as it cools the engines. The dirt, grit and sticky colloid particles in the seawater would clog the ship's pipes in a few years if it wasn't for magnetism suspending this debris so it doesn't cake inside. Farmers magnetize irrigation water because it has been proven conclusively the magnetized water germinates crops a third better than plain water, especially grains like oats, wheat and corn.

Dan Marino, Quarterback of the Miami Dolphins

"My football injury resulted in torn tendons and ligaments in my foot. I expected to miss 8 weeks of season, but doctors used Magnetic Therapy to accelerate the healing process and I returned in just 3 weeks!"

Today, nurserymen, horticulturists and gardeners regularly put new seedlings on a magnetized disc because they know a plant will grow a third faster sitting on a magnet than without. This is just one more miracle that is well-documented (try it yourself) where magnetism helps things grow.

Veterinarians, owners and trainers have been using magnetized mats on thoroughbred horses for 50 years. It helps the horses with sprains, soreness and cardiovascular stress from racing and gets them out on the track faster earning a paycheck. Trainers also use the magnetized mats on the excitable steeds when they are trailering them because the magnetization has a calming effect on these very expensive animals. The American Thoroughbred Assn. estimates that the owners of race horses spend over $2 million to keep their horses in peak racing condition through the use of magnetized blankets.

According to Dr. Gary Null in his book *Healing With Magnets,* space exploration would not be possible without the magnet energy fields. In the 1960's, when our first astronauts took off, you remember seeing the newsreel footage of the space capsules landing in the Pacific Ocean. The helicopter would pluck the capsule from he sea and deposit them on the flight deck of the nearby carrier. Naval medics would take the astronauts away on stretchers. At first it was assumed that they couldn't walk because the weightlessness of space weakened their muscles to the normal atmospheric pressure of Earth. However, upon investigation, it was found that the lack the Earth's magnetic field disrupted their muscle coordination and temporarily atrophied the strength of their muscles. To remedy this situation, all spacesuits are now sewn with small magnets dispersed throughout the suit to maintain the astronauts natural muscular equilibrium. The new space station going up will have is own magnetic generator creating a life-giving magnetic field throughout the whole station so that the workers will have the same exposure to magnetism as they enjoy down here on earth.

Dick Van Dyke, Actor
"I've had arthritis for years. I've tried every pill, nostrum,and treatment and then I tried Magnetic Field Therapy and believe it is responsible for keeping me functioning in relative comfort."

In the wonderful world of sports, magnetic devices are found everywhere from race car drivers, golfers, tennis players, wrestlers, rodeo, football, basketball, baseball, hockey, to Olympic gymnasts, track and field. Everybody wants to use magnets to enhance their performance, provide relief from training soreness, rehabilitation from injury, general wellness, greater endurance, and the overall calmness derived from magnetic therapy. We could fill the book with unpaid testimonials and endorsements from a galaxy of well-known performers in a myriad number of sports.

Probably the greatest sports story in conjunction with the healing powers of magnets is the Jim Colbert documentary. In 1994, pro-golfer Jim Colbert was forced to leave the game he loved because of the debilitating advance of osteoarthritis. His condition was so severe that he could not play 18 holes of golf, because he couldn't walk a complete round, nor swing a club, nor even tee up a golf ball on a bad day. He was totally finished from the game he so loved. Fortunately, for him, his friends and fellow pro golfers, Chi Chi Rodriguez and Bob Murphy told him about the success they enjoyed with magnetic therapy, and urged him to start using magnetic sleep pads and other magnetic products. His successful therapy was overwhelming. In 1996, he reentered the PGA Senior Tour and won it! In 1997 he won again, a two year total of $8,400,000 in purses, awards and endorsements, all from a man who was giving up golf because arthritis had crippled him to such an extent, until he discovered the miracle of magnets. With Jim Colbert as a shining example 90% of all the senior men golfers on the PGA tour go to sleep nightly on a magnetic sleep

**Jim Colbert,
Pro Golfer
Senior PGA Tour**
"In 1994, I considered myself too crippled to play golf anymore. But since starting Magnetic Therapy, I haven't missed one golf tournament that I wanted to play in.

system. They get the results. The Senior Men's PGA Tour is America's healthiest group of senior men in America, and it is no mere coincidence that they all use magnets to maintain and improve their wonderful healthy lives.

In Hollywood, aging actors are using magnets to stay in shape years after they normally would have heard their last curtain call. As we all get older no one wants to succumb to the ravages of age. We all want to maintain our lives, our flexibility and our youth for as long as possible. Life is a lot of fun as long as you are not crippled up with arthritis, cardiovascular disease and sapped of energy because of insomnia. Magnets have a long history of helping people overcome these age-associated problems. They are easy to use, they are extremely safe (as long as you are not using a pacemaker the magnets could interfere with the operation of the batteries because they increase the drainage of the electricity) and they are endorsed by a galaxy of famous individuals who testify to their effectiveness not because they are paid for their confirmation, but because they are decent people who want to share their wonderful, healthy experience so that you too can gain a healthy lifestyle.

Bob Murphy
Pro Golfer
Senior PGA Tour
You have nothing to lose and everything to gain by trying magnetic therapy.

Donna Andrews
Pro Golfer
LPGA Tour
Sleeping on magnets helped me feel well and play well

Isn't it time for you to try magnets? You have nothing to lose in using these silent healers. Many people are trying them now and getting fantastic results from their daily aches and pains, and some people are getting relief from medical situations once thought fatally irreversible. Go ahead and try, you've nothing to lose.

Andy Griffith
TV Star
Magnet therapy has allowed me to lead a full life once again.

The Silent Healer

"Healing is a matter of time, but it is also sometimes a matter of opportunity."
— Hippocrates

Since creation, we have all evolved in the Earth's magnetic field. This quiet force has effected every living thing on our planet. Magnetism has touched, controlled and manipulated all creatures on our Earthly home. From the algae in the sea, to the birds in the air and to all that roam this vast land down to you and me. Our lives rely on the delicate internal magnetic fields which stimulate our brainwaves, heartbeats and nerve impulses, permitting us to live. Our lives function beautifully in this magnetic field which cocoons the Earth because this is our placenta from which we emerged. Magnetic therapy is nothing more than utilizing magnets to restore our common birthright and continue the natural flow and rhythm that has been our guiding spirit since the dawn of time.

When we are deprived of our natural magnetic balance of life, our bodies are exposed to sickness, disorder

SUMMARY

In this chapter you will learn how magnetic therapy helps you to alleviate the problems of 25 common medical conditions. Through the easy use of magnets, you set aside these uncomfortable conditions which if unchecked may eventually become deadly. These magnetic remedies will lighten your physical sickness and restore your body and mind to holistic health.

in the warmth of healing. Magnetism, can rid ourselves of these multiple illnesses which engulf us and consume our good health. This chapter lists 25 general diseased states which rob us of our healthy vigor and the enjoyment of a balanced, wholesome livelihood.

Each of the 25 listed sicknesses will be generally explained. The following paragraphs will explain how magnetic therapy will help you overcome this illness. Finally, this will be followed by scientific evidence that will confirm the results of the beneficial application of magnetic therapy so you can research further proof of how this medical utilization of magnets may help you and your loved ones.

DISEASES

1. Alzheimer's Disease
2. Arthritis
3. Cancer
4. Circulation & Cardiovascular Disease
5. Dental Disorders
6. Diabetes
7. Earaches
8. Epilepsy
9. Eye Disorders
10. Fractures
11. Headaches
12. Infection, Inflammation & Wounds
13. Insomnia
14. Kidney Disorders
15. Liver Disorders
16. Lung Disorders
17. Mental Disorders
18. Multiple Sclerosis
19. Neuropathy
20. Pain
21. Parkinson's Disease
22. Skin Disease
23. Sprains & Tendonitis
24. Stomach Problems
25. Tuberculosis
26. Urinary Disease

ALZHEIMER'S DISEASE

Description - Alzheimer's Disease is a progressive condition in which nerve cells degenerate in the brain and the mental mass shrinks. Alzheimer's disease is now known to be responsible for 75 percent of dementia cases in those over 65 years old. Because of the increasing numbers of elderly citizens, interest and research into the causes and treatment of Alzheimer's disease have greatly expanded in recent years. The progress of the disease (which, in most cases, represents several years of intellectual and personal decline until death).

Causes: A number of theories have been proposed, ranging from the effects of a chronic infection to those of toxic poisoning by a metal such as aluminum. There is known to be a reduced level of *acetylcholine* and other brain chemicals in people with Alzheimer's disease. A genetic factor is also a possibility, and 15% of the victims of Alzheimer's disease have a family history of the disease, occasionally with a dominant pattern of inheritance (in which children with one affected parent have a 50% chance of inheriting the disease). Onset is rare before the age of 60, but thereafter increases steadily with age. Up to 30 percent of people over the age of 85 are affected.

Gene Test

Genetic scientists have recently isolated the Apolipoprotein-E genes which heredically causes Alzheimer's. You get one from each parent. Your chances are:

APO-E-4	75%
APO-E-3	35%
APO-E-2	2%

A genetic test will tell your combination.

Symptoms: This disease varies among individuals, but there are three broad stages. At first the patient notices increasing forgetfulness and compensates by writing lists or by soliciting the help of others. Problems with memory causes the patient to feel anxious and depressed.

Forgetfulness gradually shades into a second phase of severe memory loss, particularly for recent events. Victims may remember long-ago events, such as their schooldays and young adulthood, but they are unable to recall yesterday's visitors or what they saw on television. They also become disoriented as to time or place, losing their way even on familiar streets; their concentration and ability to calculate numbers declines and *dysphasia* (inability to find the right word) is noticeable. Anxiety increases, mood changes are sudden and unpredictable, and personality changes soon become apparent.

Future Dilemma
As accurate genetic testing becomes commonplace, how do we handle the results? We now know the genes for Alzheimer's and Huntington's diseases. No employer or insurance company wants these costly workers.

In the third stage, patients become severely disoriented and confused. They may also suffer from symptoms of *psychosis*, such as *hallucinations* and paranoid *delusions*. Symptoms are worsened by the patient's disorientation and memory losses and are usually most severe at night. Signs of nervous system disease begin to emerge, such as primitive *reflexes* (involuntary actions that occur normally in newborn babies) and incontinence of urine and feces. Some patients become demanding, unpleasant, and sometimes violent and lose all awareness of social norms. Some become docile and somewhat helpless. They neglect personal hygiene and may wander aimlessly. Eventually the burden for caring relatives becomes impossible, and full-time hospital care and nursing are often inevitable. Once the patient is bedridden, the complications of bedsores, feeding problems, and pneumonia make life expentancy very short.

Magnetic Therapy: There is no known cure for Alzheimer's Disease. However, magnetic therapy has helped alleviate some of the symptoms caused by this illness and magnetic therapy has shown that it lessens the severity and lengthens the lucid life of people inflicted with this terrible disease that robs people of the essence of their life...their brain.

Here are some very interesting effects that magnetic therapy has on this number one cause of dementia.

NEWS ALERT
A brand new research procedure puts microscopic, magnetized steel particles inside the brain. This does not cure, but lengthens the sane lives of Alzheimer's, Huntington's and Parkinson's patients.

The BBC News reported on December 23, 1998, that research at the Barnes-Jewish Hospital enables doctors to use MRI (magnetic resonance imaging) to scan Alzheimer patients to see the tangled plaques in their brains for a true evaluation of their disease. Previously, only an autopsy could finally confirm a diagnosis of Alzheimer's! [1] Also, at Washington University School of Medicine in St. Louis, Missouri, magnetically controlled brain surgery which could relieve some of the cranial pressure of Alheizmer's was first performed in 1998. This procedure allowed for a first ever biopsy of a living brain to positively confirm a diagnosis of Alzheimer's; plus, this new magnetic therapy could also be successfully utilized on brain tumors. [2]

1. *BBC News*, 23 December 1998
2. Owen, Lara.*Pain Free with Magnet Therapy*, Prima Health,CA, 2000

A startling discovery has been made that the high gauss magnetic blast from a MRI machine temporarily relieves the tremors from Parkinson's patients and returns Alzheimer's victims to complete lucidity for up to 24 hours after exposure. Although it is not medically understood how this magnetic therapy creates such dramatic results it is believed that the high magnetic power somehow realigns the brain activity. [3]

In another peer - reviewed, scientific journal, magnetic therapy helped Alzheimer's patients with spatial orientation, mood, social relationships, memory and other cognitive functions. [4] All of us live our lives with the *circadian rhythms* of our biological clocks. Shift workers like policemen, firemen, paramedics, etc. who work changeable hours have difficulty adjusting, relaxing and sleeping. Magnetic therapy has been found to help alleviate the memory deterioration and mood swings of such people and have helped Alzheimer's patients slow down their mental deterioration caused by their circadian rhythms being upset by their mental disease. [5]

A very wealthy Alzheimer's patient's estate was being contested by heirs. Only he could decide, but he was totally incompetent. Put into an MRI, he became totally lucid, settled the matter, had a big family dinner, slipped away and died 2 weeks later.

In Alzheimer's, the most common mineral deficiency is iron which is essential for the best cognitive function. Whereas, magnetic therapy does not supply iron to the diet, increased supplies of this mineral will be best uti-

3. Ibid
4. Sandyk, R., *International Journal of NeuroSci*, June 1994
5. Sandyk, R., *International Journal of NeuroSci*, August 1991

lized by magnetic therapy to lessen the terrible effects on the mental balance of the patient. [6]

Magnetic therapy is leading the way to helping these unfortunate Alzheimer's patients. It has slowed many of the problems suffered, but more research is necessary to stop this dreadful disease.

6. Fairbanks, U.F.; Beuther, E.; *Iron In; Modern Nutrition in Health and Disease*; Philadelphia, PA, 1988

ARTHRITIS

Description - Arthritis is the general inflammation of a joint, characterized by pain, swelling, stiffness and redness. Arthritis is not a single disorder but the name of joint disease from a number of causes. The arthritis may involve one joint or many and can vary in severity from a mild ache and stiffness to severe pain and, later, joint deformity.

Causes - *Osteoarthritis* - Also known as degenerative arthritis, this is the most common type of arthritis. It results from wear and tear on the joints, evolved in middle age, and most commonly troubles older people.

Rheumatoid Arthritis - The most severe type of inflammatory joint disease, this is an *autoimmune disorder* in which the body's *immune system* acts against and damages joints and surrounding soft tissues. Many joints - most commonly those in the hands, feet, and arms - become extremely painful, stiff and deformed.

Rheumatoid arthritis is an autoimmune disease because the immune system attacks itself. Lupus, MS, Type 1 diabetes, Graves and fibromyalgia are others. These affect women more than twice as much as men. Science don't know why.

Still's Disease - Juvenile rheumatoid arthritis; it is most common in children under the age of 4. It usually clears up after a few years, but even then may stunt growth and leave the child with permanent deformities.

Sero-negative arthritis - This is a group of disorders

that causes symptoms and signs of arthritis in a number of joints, although blood test results for rheumatoid arthritis are negative. It can be associated with skin disorders *(psoriasis)*, inflammatory intestinal disorders *(Crohn's disease)*, or autoimmune disorders.

Ineffective arthritis - Also known as septic or pyogenic arthritis, this is joint disease caused by the invasion of bacteria into the joint from a nearby infected wound or from *bacteremia* (infection in the bloodstream). The infected joint usually becomes hot as well as painful and swollen. Arthritis may also occur as a complication of an infection elsewhere in the body, such as *chickenpox, rubella* (German measles), *mumps, rheumatic fever,* or *gonorrhea;* it may also be a complication of *nonspecific urethritis,* in which case the joint inflammation forms part of *Reiter's syndrome.*

Ankylosing spondylitis - In this arthritis of the spine, the joints linking the vertebrae become inflamed and the vertebrae fuse. The arthritis may spread to other joints, often the hips and is extremely painful.

Gout is usually depicted by a fat, wealthy man with his foot up on a pillow. His problem is too much blood urine forming uric crystals in his big toe. This very painful condition can be helped by magnetic therapy.

Gout - This disorder is associated with a form of arthritis in which uric acid (one of the body's waste products) accumulates in joints in the form of crystals, causing inflammation. It usually affects one joint at a time.

Symptoms: The diagnosis is made from the patient's symptoms and signs. To discover the cause, fluid may be withdrawn through a needle from an affected joint. This fluid may then be examined microscopically for the presence of microorganisms, or uric acid or other crystals. Sometimes a *culture* is made from the fluid so that it can be analyzed for any infection.

MRI imaging may be carried out to reveal the type and extent of damage to joints. Blood tests can reveal the presence of proteins typical of rheumatoid arthritis, a high level of uric acid indicative of gout or sometimes a high ESR (erythrocyte sedimentation rate), indicating inflammation.

Magnetic Therapy: Again, just like with Alzheimer's there is presently no cure for arthritis; however, magnetic therapy has dramatic results in reducing the pain and inflammation associated with the many forms of arthritis and is thus an invaluable tool to the arthritis sufferer.

The 100 different forms of arthritis are America's #1 crippling disease. One out of every seven people suffer from the pain, stiffness and swelling of this joint disease. Magnet therapy helps tremendously.

According to *USA Today,* there are 66 million Americans who suffer some form and to some degree from arthritis, and roughly 33% have altered their lifestyle because of the pain. [7] Therefore, it is a major problem and although not a cure, magnetic therapy helps dramatically to relieve the associated pain and allow people to live normal, productive lives. Magnetic therapy, coupled with proper nutrition and regular exercise is a winning natural alternative to the often prescribed prescription medications that too many arthritis sufferers are given by their doctors.[8]

7. USA Today, *Arthritis is a Growing American Problem*, Dec. 6, 1996.

8. U.S. News & World Report, *Prescription Medicines are a Problem*, Feb. 19, 2001.

In the *Journal of Rheumatology*, a double-blind, randomized trial using magnetic therapy on people suffering from arthritis of the knee was tested using 6 variables of motion and discomfort. At the end of the month, the group having magnets imbedded in their knee braces had improvements from 23 to 61 percent. The group who had plastic inserts in their knee braces reported improvements of only 2 to 18 percent. The decreased pain and better motion indicates that magnetic therapy helps arthritis sufferers. [9] Another similar study was conducted the next year in Europe, and the results were similar. [10]

In another test of children aged 7 to 14 years old suffering from juvenile rheumatoid arthritis the results showed positive results with the application of magnetic field therapy. [11] In a Russian test on adults with rheumatoid arthritis, exposure of two weeks to magnetic therapy brought an astounding 90% relief to the patients. [12] In an Italian research on magnetic therapy with people suffering from arthritis of the hand, there was a significant improvement over 4 weeks. [13]

Artificial joints first had widespread use after WW II. Today, 250,000 arthritis sufferers get new joints and hips. Modern replacements are computer designed for the best prostheses.
Human Anatomy, 1992

9. Miner, W.K.; Markoll, R., *Journal of Rheumatolgy*, 1993.

10. Trock, D.H.; et al; *Journal of Rheumatology*, 1994

11. Lawrence, R.; Rosch, P.J.; *Magnet Therapy, the Pain Cure Alternative*, Prima Health, CA, 1998.

12. Shlyapok, E.A.; et al; *Vopr Kurortol Fizioter Lech Fiz Kult*, 1992

13. Zizic, T.; et al; *Second World Congress for Electricity and Magnetism in Biology and Medicine*, Bologna, Italy, June, 8-13, 1997

CANCER

Description: Cancer is a disease that has affected humans since prehistoric times and is also common in domestic and farm animals, birds and fish. Apart from childhood cancers, which may be associated with events during pregnancy, such as exposure to radiation, most cancers are a feature of aging. Cancer is a group of diseases in which symptoms are due to the unrestrained growth of cells in one of the body organs or tissues. Most commonly, malignant tumors develop in major organs, such as the lungs, breasts, intestines, skin, stomach, or pancreas, but they may also develop in the nasal sinuses, testes, ovaries, lips, or tongue. Cancers may also develop in the blood cell-forming tissues of the bone marrow (the *leukemias*) and in the lymphatic system, muscles, or bones. Cancer is the second most common cause of death in the US, accounting for about one-fifth of the total (the most common is heart disease).

Cancer Causing Agents
1. Natural (sun, smog, pollutants, food poisons 35%
2. Tobacco smoke 30%
3. Sexual activity 7%
4. Occupational 4%
5. Alcohol 3%
6. Food additives 1%
7. Unknown causes 20%

Cancers are not the only type of abnormal growth, or *neoplasm*, that occur in the body. However, a cancer differs from a *benign* tumor, such as a wart or a *lipoma*, in two important ways. As it grows, it spreads and infiltrates the tissues around it and may block passageways, destroy nerves, and erode bone. Cells from the cancer may spread via the blood vessels and lymphatic channels to other parts of the body, where these metastases form new, satellite tumors that grow independently.

Causes - The growth of a cancer begins when the *oncogenes* (genes controlling cell growth and multiplication) in a cell or cells are transformed by agents known as *carcinogens*.

Once a cell is transformed into a tumor-forming type, the change in its oncogenes is passed on to all offspring cells. A small group of abnormal cells is established, and they divide more rapidly than the normal surrounding cells. Usually the abnormal cells show a lack of *differentiation* - they no longer perform the specialized task of the cells of their host tissue - and may escape the normal control of hormones and nerves. They are in effect parasites, contributing nothing to their host tissue but continuing to consume nutrients (like the visiting brother-in-law).

Years may pass before the growth of cells becomes large enough to cause symptoms, although the rate of growth varies according to the tissue or origin. Current estimates suggest that some cancers of the lung and breast have been present for more than five years before they cause symptoms. During this "occult" phase, metastases may be seeded in the liver, lungs, bones, or brain, and, in these circumstances, surgical cure is impossible because the cancer has already spread far beyond the primary site or origin.

Symptoms - The range of symptoms that may be produced by cancers is vast, depending on the site of the growth, the tissue of origin, and the extent of the growth. Symptoms may be a direct feature of the growth (e.g., lumps or skin changes) or derived from obstruction or bleeding into passageways such as the lung airways, gastrointestinal tract, or urinary tract, or from disruption of the function of a vital organ. Tumors pressing on or disturbing nerve tracts can cause nervous system disorders and pain. Some tumors lead to the overproduction of hormones with complications and effects far distant from the site of the growth. Unexplained weight loss is a feature of many types of cancer.

Types of Cancer Tests

Types	Method
Cytology	Pap Smear
	Urine Analysis
Imaging	X-rays, MRI
Chemical	Fecal Bicod
	Blood enzymes
Direct	Endoscope
	tProstate probe

Some important warning signals that always warrant investigation by a physician are shown in the accompanying table.

Magnetic Therapy: Modern medical science is making a huge headway in curing many types of cancer and today, in America, about half are cured into permanent remission. The survival rates from diagnosis to death are longer and longer. Cancer is no longer an automatic "kiss of death" our grandparents feared. Magnetic therapy is not a single remedy for cancer, but for many types it is an important contributor to a patient's remission and survival equation.

In an extraordinary application of magnetic therapy, Dr. John Pole of the Pediatric Hematology-Oncology Dept. of the University of Florida School of Medicine injected magnetic particles into extracted bone marrow. The cancerous cells miraculously adhered to the magnetic bits which was than strained away leaving only cancer-free bone marrows to be reintroduced into the child's body, thus saving this child from deadly leukemia. [14]

Dr. Robert Seeger of the University of Southern California School of Medicine performed the same type of magnetic therapy on a two-year-old child with a neuroblastoma (a cancerous tumor in the adrenal gland). Usually, 90% of children die from this cancer, but again the magnetized particles "pulled" the cancerous malignancy out of the adrenals and saved the child. [15]

In Sweden, Dr. Goesta Wollin used 4,000 gauss magnets manufactured in Japan by Sumitomo Special Metals Company to destroy breast cancer tumors. [16] Also, from Sweden, Dr. Bjorn Nordenstrom used magnetic therapy to cure a patient of metastic lung cancer and presented his report at the First International (Montreaux) Congress in Stress in Switzerland in 1988. [17]

14. Birla, G.S. and Hemlin, C.; *Magnet Therapy*, Healing Arts Press, Rochester, Vermont 1999
15. Ibid
16. Wollin, G. and Euby, E.; *Curing Cancer with Supermagnets*, Chalmers University Press; Goteborg, Sweden, 1987
17. Lawrence, R., Rosch, P.J., and Plowden, J., *Magnet Therapy, The Pain Cure Alternative*, Prima Health, CA, 1998

Mexican cardiologist Dr. Demetrio Sodi-Pullares, used magnetic therapy to rid a heart tissue from cancer by application of a polarizing magnetic solution and his report was presented in 1996 at the North American Academy of Magnetic Therapy Annual meeting. [18]

Dr. Yushio Manaka of the American Association of Oriental Medicine has found that acupuncture helps prevent the onset of cancerous tumors. [19] In Japan, Dr. Y. Omote found that magnetic therapy interrupted the cancer's progression to the point where the cancer cells went from proliferation to a nonpro-liferation phase.

Cancer is a part of life's processes. It occurs when normal cell divisions go away and produce an abnormal cell. Not all are bad, many are benign (kindly). Almost half of Americans will develop malignant (bad) cancer and 20% will die.

In Russia, Dr. N. G. Bakhmutski used magnetic therapy on a 48-year-old woman with breast cancer, and after 60 one hour exposures to magnetic therapy her breast cancer nodes disappeared, and all traces of cancer disappeared after an additional 50 treatments. [20] Also, in the Ukraine, Dr. D. V. Miasoedov had an 87% success rate in forcing cancer into remission by the use of magnetic exposure by a high powered MRI machine. He worked with patients suffering from a variety of cancers. [21] Again in Russia, Dr. L.S. Ogorodnikova reported treating lung cancer patients to 20-30 magnetic therapy sessions with positive effect of tumor remission. [22] Dr. V.G. Andreev worked

18. Ibid
19. Manaka, Yushio; *Chasing the Dragon's Tail*, Paradign Press, Brookline, Mass., 1995
20. Omote, Y., *Nippon Geka Gakkai Zasshi*, Japan, 198821. Bakhmutski, N.G.; et al., *Soviet Medicine*, Moscow, USSR, 1991
22. Miasoedov, D.V., et al.; Abstracts of the First All-Union Symposium with International Participation; Kiev, Ukraine, 1989

with throat cancer patients whom he exposed to 3,000 gauss magnetic therapy. The results were excellent. [23]

23. Andreev, V.G., et al.; *Effect of a Constant Magnetic Field as Therapy with Patients with Cancer of the Throat*, Fizicheskaia Meditaina, Moscow, 1994.

CIRCULATION & CARDIOVASCULAR DISEASE

Description- The heart and blood vessels, which together are responsible for the continuous flow of blood throughout the body. Also called the cardiovascular system, the circulatory system provides all body tissues with a regular supply of oxygen and nutrients and carries away carbon dioxide and other waste products.

The circulatory system consists of two main parts: the systemic circulation (whole body, except lungs) and the pulmonary circulation to the lungs.

The systemic circulation begins at the left side of the heart, where the left atrium receives oxygen-rich blood from the pulmonary circulation. The blood is ejected from the left atrium to the left ventricle, a powerful pump that sends the blood out through the *aorta,* the body's main artery. Other arteries branching off the aorta carry the blood all over the body, into the arterioles (small arteries) that supply the various organs. The arterioles branch further into a network of capillaries. These extremely fine blood vessels have thin walls to allow oxygen and other nutrients to pass easily from the blood into the tissues, and carbon dioxide and other wastes to pass in the opposite direction.

Body Electric
Electricity is constantly flowing from the static, ionic charge created by your blood flow. This electrical charge beats your heart, stimulates your nerves and allows you to think.
Dr. M. Molesky - MIT

The capillaries deliver the deoxygenated blood into venules (small veins), which join to form veins. These carry the blood into the *venae cavae,* which then return the blood to the right atrium.

From the right atrium, the blood enters the pulmonary circulation. It passes to the right ventricle, which pumps the blood through the pulmonary artery to the lungs. Here, carbon dioxide passes out of the blood, and oxygen enters. The reoxygenated blood then returns through the pulmonary veins to the left atrium of the heart, where it reenters the systemic circulation.

Within the systemic circulation there is a bypass to the liver called the portal circulation. Capillaries carrying nutrient-rich blood from the stomach, intestine, and other digestive organs join to form venules which, in turn, meet to form veins. These then merge to form the portal vein, which conveys the blood to veins, venules, and capillaries in the liver.

On its journey from the heart to the tissues, blood is forced along the arteries at high pressure. However, on the return journey through the veins and back to the heart, the blood is at low pressure. It is kept moving by the muscles in the veins preventing the blood from flowing backward.

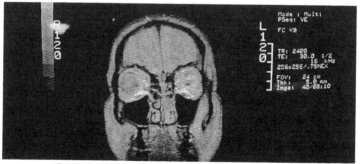

CAT Scan of blood flow thru the brain.

Causes - The circulatory is the dominant biological system in your body. Your life hangs in a critical 15 minute balance; if it falters, it's fatal. It is in constant motion and has the greatest vulnerability for breakdown; It deserves your utmost attention for it is the true barometer of your overall health. When we discuss the application of magnetic therapy we will dissect the possibilities of what can go wrong with the multiple functions of this river of life that courses through your body.

We all think of the heart and blood as the pump and transportation system that brings life-giving oxygen and nutrients to our gasping, starving trillions of cells. It does do that, but it does a lot more. Your nervous system is generally considered your communications network but your blood transports hormones and neurotransmitters which tell your far flung organs what to do, how to do it and when you should do it. It tells you fright, or to flight, or to stand and fight, and if you get these signals confused you might wind up as the lion's lunch.

The River of Life
Blood accounts for 8% of your body weight. It is slightly alkaline (7.4-pH) to counter the acidity of nutrients and its saltiness is the same as seawater.

The average body has 10 pints of blood. Your heart pumps this blood through your cardiovascular system every minute...while you are sleeping! When you are awake, and running the maze of life between work, home and play (hopefully); your little 4 cylinder motor is pumping out at 40 pints a minute. With quick math, you are circulating your blood through your whole cardiovascular system at an astonishing 15 seconds at speeds of up to 100 mph (and you didn't think you got around much).

41

This bloody merry-go-round is generating a lot of heat. That's why you are 98.6° F 24 hrs. a day, 7 days a week, 365 days a year (women are usually 98.7° - they have two layers of fat and 10% more water than men - they are hotter and wetter) since the day you were born. If you went out to garden, or play golf or even take a bath and it was 98° F, you would feel warm. We are burning up from the friction of our blood racing through our bodies, that is why we eat so much.

More important than the heat that is generated by this friction, is the electricity that it generates. You are literally a human dynamo pumping up the juice. Your brain and nervous system need this electricity in order to operate. Your brain is the equivalent of a 40 watt light bulb.

Symptoms - If your generating system slows down as it usually does after your 45th birthday candle is blown out, you start to develop all types of age-associated problems which stem from the fact that your circulatory system is not flowing at full capacity. Simple things start to happen like your feet get cold when you are sleeping and your once vibrant handshake now feels like an old, dead clam. More important is that your 40 watt lightbulb/brain no longer shines so brightly because its been downsized to a 35 watt on a rolling brownout headed for old-aged senility and dementia. Alzheimer's is the #1 worry of

America's rapidly aging Baby Boomer population, but in reality the slowing of your blood flow through your circulatory system is the much greater cause of you forgetting your anniversary or where you put your house keys.

CLAUDICATION
Means lameness or limping. The term is associated with the Roman Emperor Claudius, who was notably lame. As a medical term it refers to a cramplike pain in one or both legs, which develops when walking and may eventually cause a limp. The usual cause of claudication is atherosclerosis.

Magnetic Therapy - It is often debated among doctors who understand the biological effects of magnetic therapy (they are few and far between because American medical schools do not teach natural health alternatives because our medical profession is almost totally involved with the fast-acting, reactive medical procedures of surgery and pharmaceutical prescriptions to bother learning about proactive, natural health alternatives that will gently maintain your personal health, wellness and longevity) whether it's best use is for improved circulation or pain management. My opinion is to concentrate our magnetic therapy emphasis on circulation of the cardiovascular system because increased oxygenation of the blood reduces soreness, inflammation and infections; thus, you have less pain.

All atoms have positive or negative charges, and these charged atomic ions play a critical role in the circulation of our blood. Not that you necessarily want to taste your blood unless you are from Transylvania and not Pennsylvania, but it tastes salty (taste your tears or perspiration, it is all salty). This is because the positive sodium ions (Na+) and the negative chlorine ions (CI-)

have a magnetic attraction for each other (opposites attract - remember the first rule of magnetism). This sodium salt combines with potassium, calcium and water to form a saline solution which comprises over half of your blood supply. This saline solution is mixed with proteins, hormones, fats (lipids and cholesterol), glucose (many types of sugars) and immunological factors make up your plasma. The saline solution is responsible for the rhythm stimulation of your heart (the beat goes on...hopefully), regulates your water balance (tells you when you have to go), contracts your muscles (no salt - no walk) and conducts nerve impulses throughout your body from your brain (if you lose too much salt through perspiration loss on a desert trek you will feel faint or worse, go into a coma). People who go overboard on a salt-free diet don't move around a lot and miss out on a lot of fun.

Your blood is slightly negatively charged and your arterial walls (the basic pipes of your personal plumbing) are also negatively charged (remember the second rule of magnetism is that like charges repel each other). The fact that your blood and the pipes that carry the flow are of the same charge is beneficial because it keeps the blood (which tends to be gooey and sticky as you get older) from adhering to the sides of the cardiovascular plumbing. This negative charge of your arterial walls diminishes as you age (like everything else). This is real bad for you.

Navy with Magnetized Pipes

In 1903, seawater used to cool the engines was clogging the pipes with salts. The Navy found by magnetizing the seawater, the salts would not stick to the insides of the pipes.

Dr. Roger Coghill

When the lessening of the negative charge of your plumbing occurs, blood starts to stick to the walls of your arteries. This situation leads to atherosclerosis, which leads to more deaths of Americans than any other causes. The fatty plaques that form on the inner walls of the arteries are caused by a host of factors. Contributing factors are a diet of junk food with a heavy emphasis on sugars, fats and chemical preservatives which often act as binding agents (glue) which help the plaque stick to your arteries and not get flushed along with the speedy blood flow (often moving at 100 mph). Other critical factors are cigarette smoking (an astounding 90% of tobacco junkies develop atherosclerosis). Additional causes are stress causing hypertension and medically inadequately controlled diabetes. When atherosclerosis develops in the torso or limbs it is called *Peripheral Vascular Disease*, in the heart it is called *Coronary Heart Disease*, in the lungs, *Pulmonary Embolism* and in the brain, *Stroke* - they all are fatal and kill more Americans than any other biological cause of death.

As this plaque builds up in the arteries and veins the first signs are usually an aching, tired feeling in the leg muscles when walking. It occurs mostly in the calf but may be felt anywhere in the leg. Typically the pain is relieved by resting the leg for a few minutes but recurs after roughly the same amount of walking as before. This symptom is called intermittent *claudication*. Prolonged use of the arms may produce a similar symptom.

As the disease worsens, the amount of activity possible before symptoms develop decreases, until eventually pain is present at rest. This pain may be severe and continuous, disturbing sleep; to relieve it, the sufferer may dangle the limb over the edge of the bed. At this

stage, an affected leg is dangerously short of blood supply; the foot and lower leg are cold and often numb, the skin is dry and scaly, and *leg ulcers* tend to develop after minor injury. In the final stage there is gangrene which usually starts in the toes and then spreads upward.

In severe cases in which gangrene has developed, amputation is necessary, usually to just below the knee to leave a suitable stump for fitting an artificial limb.

Sometimes, sudden arterial blockage occurs. It may be caused by a clot developing rapidly on top of a plaque of atherosclerosis, be a dissecting *aneurysm* (splitting of an arterial wall), or by an *embolism* arising from a clot formed in the heart and carried to obstruct a peripheral artery. Blockage causes sudden severe pain in the affected limb, which becomes cold and either pale or blue. There is no pulse in the limb, and movement and sensation in it are lost. Another sure sign of atherosclerosis is a rising blood pressure as the blockage grows narrowing the diameter of the shrinking artery.

Iatrogenic Injuries
In America, we are very smug in our belief that we have the best medicine - but do we? According to the Journal of the American Medical Association, our medical establishment kills over 180,000 Americans per year (this is what is reported, the actual number is surely much higher for physicians fear malpractice) through Iatrogenic Injuries (means doctor caused). Every day 500 Americans die in our hospitals because of misdiagnosed medicine.
JAMA 1997

Magnetic Therapy - Dr. Philpott describes a 70-year-old man who continued to suffer pain after undergoing coronary bypass surgery. He lived in chronic depression, walked in a labored shuffle and talked with noticeable slurring. After sleeping on a magnetized sleep system for only one month, the man's depressed symptoms vanished and he returned to normalcy. [24]

24. Philpott, W. and Taplin, S.; *Biomagnetic Handbook*, Enviro-Tech, Choctak, OK, 1990

Another 46-year-old man suffered for years from a severe heart flutter which caused him nausea and diarrhea complications. No treatment seemed to help until Dr.

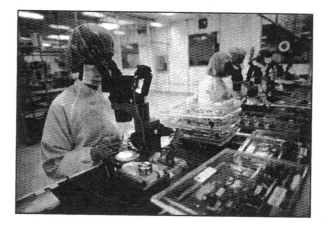

Ludwig of San Martino, Italy used magnetic therapy. His severe cardiac arrhythmia soon ceased and never returned. [25] Arrhythmia is a disorder where the electrical current to the heart is interfered with and the normal transmission of impulses becomes erratic. There are two types of arrhythmia: *sinus bradycardia* and *atrial fibrillation*. Both types are affected by magnetic therapy and the method of remedy is that magnetic energy has been proven many times to smooth out and restore normal flow of electrical atoms (electric current). [26]

Serious study of magnetic therapy started at the beginning of the 20th century. A Dutch physicist, Dr. Heike Kamerlingh of Groningen, the Netherlands, discovered

25. Goldberg, B.; *Alternative Medicine*, Future Medicine Publishing, Fife, WA, 1995
26. American Medical Association, *The AMA Encyclopedia*, Random House, N.Y.C., NY, 1989

the phenomenon of superconductivity of magnetism and electricity. Without this research, magnetism could not be measured. He was awarded the Nobel Prize for Physics in 1913 for his cutting edge research. [27]

The study of magnetic therapy as it coordinates with the body was first discovered by Otto Stern, an American naturalized German physicist who in 1921 discovered the magnetic property of atoms with his magneton. This research was continued by G.H. Baule and R. McFee who succeeded in making the first magneto cardiogram in 1962, which developed into both the electrocardiogram (ECG- for measuring heart waves) and electroeucephalography (EEG - for measuring brain waves). Both of these life-saving diagnostic machines would not have been developed nor possible if it were not for the inspired scientific exploration of magnetic therapy. [28]

Probably the greatest award bestowed to magnetic therapy research was the Nobel Prize given to Dr. Linus C. Pauling in 1954 for his breakthrough research on the magnetic properties of hemoglobin. His crucial discovery explained how the body breathes and distributes oxygen throughout. Prior to his discovery, we did not know how the human body utilized oxygen, all we knew was that if we didn't breathe, we would be dead in 15 minutes. Dr. Pauling, a chemist, discovered that iron has a very strong magnetic attraction of oxygen and that one iron atom could hold 4 oxygen atoms. Utilizing this natural law of science, Dr. Pauling found that the body's iron was contained in the hemoglobin in the red blood cells

27. Crystal, D.; Biographical Encyclopedia, Cambridge University Press, Cambridge, England, UK, 1998
28. Birla, S.G. and Hemlin, D.; *Magnet Therapy*, Healing Arts Press, Rochester, VT, 1999

and through the passage of blood through the lungs it picked up the oxygen and following the cardiovascular pathways distributed this oxygen to the cells to be used to convert food into energy through oxidation. We see this iron/oxygen event everyday - it is called "rust." [29]

In Russian medicine, they did not have the research funds nor the capitalistic urgency to generate profits, so their medical technology did not evolve around the prescription medications which so prevade American medicine. Their medical experimentation was wholly underwritten by the government and they believed, as many countries do (especially the Japanese) that magnetic therapy research is worthwhile. Therefore, we have many scientific studies from Russia which are very valid. Much of the American medical community makes fun of the Russians, but their scientists, engineers and physicians (half are women, gender equality is much greater there) are really top notch. Remember, they were the first to put a satellite, a human and live aboard station into space.

Bigger is Not Better
A 150 lb. man has 10 pints of blood. A 300 lb. man only has 12 pints. A new theory on why bigger, fatter people die sooner is that their body is stressed by lack of circulation. Rarely do 200 lb. people under 6' live past 70.

In one study, a patient's heart was not receiving enough blood and ischemic heart disease was soon to claim its victim. Magnetic therapy restored normal flow and the patient was saved. [30]

29. Barnes-Svarney, P., *The N.Y. Public Library Science Desk Reference*, Simon & Schuster, MacMillan, N.Y.C., NY, 1995
30. Vasileva, E.M., et al., Vopr Kurortol Fizioter Lech Fiz Kult, Moscow, 1994

Twenty-three children with irregular cardiac rhythm returned to normal when magnetic therapy was insturmental in synchronizing the beat. [31]

Children with primary arterial hypertension and vagotonic symptoms returned to normal under the beneficial influence of magnetic therapy. [32]

In England, studies done on atherosclerosis showed that arterial plaques were resolved by use of magnetic therapy. [33]

In Italy, magnetic therapy increased microcirculation in state II hypertension patients. [34] Animal studies on rats and rabbits showed magnetic therapy renewed hearts that had suffered myocardium infarcts. [35] Thirty myocardial patients received magnetic therapy along with millimeter-wave treatments (MW), another thirty only received MW treatment. The group who had magnetic therapy recuperated twice as fast. [36]

In Germany, a double-blind, placebo-controlled study tested a group suffering from dizziness, headache, cardiodynia and hypertension was treated with magnetic

31. Kirillova, Y.B., et al., *Vopr Kurortol Fizioter Lech Fiz Kult*, Moscow, 1992
32. Zadionchenko, V.S., et al., *Vopr Kurortol Fizioter Lech Fiz Kult*, Moscow, 1994
33. Gordon, R.T. and D., *Medical Hypotheses*, London, Feb. 1981
34. Cadossi, R.; *Second World Congress for Magnetism*, Bologna, June 1997
35. Gahelina, I.E.; et al., *Millimetrovie Volni v. Biologi I Meditcine*, Rome, 1994
36. Naumcheva, N.N., *Millimetrovie Volni v. Biologi I Mediticine*, Rome, 1994

therapy, the others were not treated. The group with magnetic therapy got better in half the time. [37]

The Washington Post reported that in the town of Tlacole, Mexico, many people with cardiovascular, digestive and kidney problems travel for miles to drink the highly magnetic water which naturally flows in this place from mountain springs. Many report "miraculous" benefits from drinking this magnetized water.

All over the world, people report amazing results from magnetic therapy... how about you?

37. Budkar, L.N.; et al., *Doktor Lending*, Germany, 1996

DENTAL DISORDERS

Description - Many people do not adequately pay attention to their teeth and periodontal health. This is a major mistake for 85% of all the infections of your body enter through your mouth. If you protect the largest orifice from bacterial, viral and fungal invasion you will go a long way to protecting your whole body. Your mouth is your gateway to your body and it is a prudent idea to close the gate.

Causes - If you don't brush and floss your teeth regularly, and go to a dentist at least once a year for a cleaning you allow plaque to build up at the base of your teeth. This plaque is made up of bacteria, lactic acid and food debris. Left on your teeth, it dissolves the dental calcium coating and starts tooth decay. Even more serious than tooth decay, where your health liability is that all you will lose in your teeth, as the dental plaque accumulates, it calcifies, forming cal-

WARNING
Ever read the warning on the tube of toothpaste. It is as strongly worded as cigarette warnings and rightly so. The fluoride used in the average tube is enough to kill a child. Fluoride is a strong poison, be careful!

culus (Latin for "stone") or tartar (named after the fierce Asian invaders of Rome, you guessed it, they had bad teeth. When this happens, the calculus/tartar pries the gums away from the base of the teeth and your health liability becomes the real potential of losing your life through bacterial invasion of your cardiovascular system. [38] This event leads to peridontal disease which effects 80% of Americans over the age of 55.

38. Marieb, Elaine N., *Human Anatomy and Physiology*, Benjamin/ Cummings Publishi8ng, Redwood City, CA 1995

Symptoms - Your mouth is a real breeding ground for hundreds of different types of bacteria, which serve the beneficial purposes of killing toxic bacterial invaders which come in with your food and drink and they also help with digestion of your food. Your mouth was designed to accommodate these beneficial visitors and as long as they stay in your mouth all is A-OK. However, when the plaque opens up spaces between your teeth and gums through periodontal disease, you have got a prison break going on in your mouth. The convict bacteria then go from your mouth where they are kept under control, into your bloodstream through the open sores in your gums. Now, you are in a world of trouble. Two of the most common bacteria in your mouth are gingivitis and streptococcal bacteria. [39] In the mouth they are not only harmless, but beneficial as mercenaries killing other bacteria. However, once these desperadoes get into your bloodstream, they turn on their host.

The gingivitis is particularly deadly because once it gets into your bloodstream it heads straight for your heart. The gingivitis loves to burrow into the heart muscle; especially, the heart valves where it causes *endocarditis*.[40] As your heart weakens with the gingivitis infection of your *endocardia muscle* you have symptoms of fatigue, feverishness, night sweats and vague aches and pains all because you didn't brush your teeth regularly.

The streptococci bacteria is less deadly than the gingivitis, but it causes a wider variety of health problems.

39. American Medical Assn.; *The AMA Encyclopedia*, Random House, N.Y.C., NY, 1989
40. IBID

The streptococci bacteria is definitely on the FBI's Most Wanted List as a dangerous felon! It causes strep throat (its namesake crime), tonsillitis, otitis media (middle ear infection), pneumonia, scarlet fever, urinary tract infections, and recent research suspects that streptococci can be responsible for the problems with Alzheimer's.

Magnetic Therapy - The Periodontics Division of the Medical University of South Carolina in 1998 conducted research into the efficacy of magnetized water on periodontal disease. They tested it on three gum problems: plaque formation, calculus buildup and gingival disease. The results of the double-blind, placebo-controlled, crossover study were amazing. The group using the magnetized water over the plain tap water users had a 64% less calculus buildup. On the original gingival disease there was a 27% beneficial lowering of incidence, but on the plaque formation the difference was negligible. [41] Plaque formation is easily controlled by simple, daily toothbrushing; but, the other two are much more detrimental to your health once they have gotten started destroying your health.

DANGER
Open Mouth
Pneumonia, a top killer of older people is often contracted because the person is breathing through their mouth and drawing air over the hundreds of bacteria, spreading them down on the unprotected lung below. This is a major cause of pneumonia. Always breathe thru your nose.

In another similar study conducted at George Mason University in Fairfax, Virginia by doctors Dan Watt and Cecilia Rosenfelder, they did a double-blind trial on 54 patients who suffered from severe plaque buildup. They

41. Johnson, K., et al., *The Effectiveness of Magnetized Water Oral Irrigation on Plaque, Calculus and Gingival Health*, Journal of Clinical Periodontal, 1998.

used a Hydrofloss oral irrigation device and each day the patients used magnetized water on their gums. The results were overwhelmingly positive that magnetized water not only keeps the pipes on U.S. Navy ships, but it will also keep your personal pipes clean and disease-free. [42]

A formal study on the use of magnetic therapy on dental patients undergoing very painful oral surgery was conducted by oral surgeon Dr. Jack P. Price. He found that when working on the hard palate, patients would require up to six injections of painkilling drugs like novocaine, realizing that administrating this much toxic pharmaceuticals so close to the brain cavity could be detrimental to the patients well being. Dr. Price experimented with magnetic therapy to lessen the amounts of drugs necessary to keep the patient calm during the oral surgery. He soon discovered that the patients felt much less pain with the application of magnetic therapy and therefore he needed to use less drugs. [43]

Patients recovering from oral surgery because of periodontal disease often have pain for a month or more following the operation. L.C. Rhodes, D.D.S. used magnetic therapy on his postoperative patients and the results were amazingly trouble-free recoveries. He attributes these results totally on the application of magnetic therapy. [44]

The Mouth
In man, the gateway to the Soul; in women, the outlet of the heart.
Will Rogers

42. Watt, D.L., Rosenfelder, C., et al., *The Effect of Oral Irrigation with a Magnetic Water Device on Plaque and Calculus*, Journal of Clinical Periodontal, 1993
43. Prince, J.P., *The Use of Low Strength Magnets on EAV Points*, American Journal of Acupuncture, 1983
44. Rhodes, L.C., *The Admunctive Utilization of Magnetic Therapy in Accelerating Tissue Healing in Oral Surgery*, National Dental Assn. Quarterly, 1981

Dr. V. Hillier found that patients suffering from various oral diseases recovered much more rapidly when magnetic therapy was used in conjunction with standard periodontal remedies. [45]

Beware of Amalgams
Silver fillings are 50% mercury and are very dangerous because through chewing you are constantly releasing mercury oxide gas which is highly poisonous and causes many physical problems if it gets into your blood supply.

45. Hillier, V., et al., *Magnetic Therapy as an Additional Therapy for Oral Diseases*, European Bioelectromagnetics Assn., Brussels, Belgium, 1992

DIABETES

Description - A disorder in which the pancreas produces insufficient or no insulin, the hormone responsible for the absorption of glucose into cells for their energy needs, and into the liver and fat cells for storage. As a result, the level of glucose in the blood becomes abnormally high, causing excessive urination and constant thirst and hunger. The body's inability to store or use glucose causes weight loss and fatigue. Diabetes also results in disordered lipid metabolism and accelerated degeneration of small blood vessels.

There are two main types of diabetes. Insulin-dependent (type I) diabetes, the more severe form, usually first appears in people under the age of 35 and most commonly in people between the ages of 10 and 16. It develops rapidly. The insulin-secreting cells in the pancreas are destroyed, probably as a result of an *immune response* after a virus infection, and insulin production ceases almost completely. Without regular injections of insulin, the sufferer lapses into a coma and dies.

The other main type, non-insulin-dependent (type II) diabetes, is usually of gradual onset and occurs mainly in people over 40. In many cases it is discovered only during a routine medical examination. Insulin is produced, but not enough to meet the body's needs, especially when the person is overweight. Often the body is resistant to the effects of insulin. In most cases, insulin-replacement injections are not required; the combination of dietary measures, weight reduction, and oral medication keeps

58

LIVING WITH DIABETES

As the level of glucose in the blood rises, the volume of urine required to carry it out of the body is increased, causing not only a continuous need to urinate but also constant thirst. The high levels of sugar in the blood and urine impair the body's ability to fight infection, leading to urinary tract infections such as cystitis and pyelonephritis), vaginal yeast infections (candidiasis), and recurrent skin infections.

Because the body's cells are starved of glucose, the sufferer feels weak and fatigued. The cells are able to obtain some energy from the breakdown of stored fat, resulting in weight loss. However, the chemical processes involved in the breakdown of fat are defective (especially in insulin-dependent diabetics), leading to the production of acids and substances called ketones, which can cause coma and sometimes death.

Other possible symptoms of undiagnosed diabetes include blurred vision, boils, increased appetite, and tingling and numbness in the hands and feet.

Symptoms develop in all untreated insulin-dependent diabetics, but symptoms develop in only one third of those with the non-insulin-dependent type. There are many people suffering from a mild form of the disease who are unaware of it. The disease often is diagnosed only after complications of the diabetes have been detected.

the condition under control.

Causes - Diabetes mellitus tends to run in families. However, of those who inherit the genes responsible for the insulin-dependent form, only a very small proportion eventually develop the disease. In these cases the disorder possibly occurs as the delayed result of a viral infection that had damaged the pancreas several years earlier.

In the case of type II dependent diabetes, the greater proportion of people predisposed to the disease by heredity (primarily those who are overweight) go on to acquire it.

Although obesity is the primary cause of unmasking latent diabetes, other causes that can unmask or aggravate diabetes are certain illnesses (among them *pancreatitis* and *thyrotoxicosis*), certain drugs (including some corticosteroids and some diuretics), infections, and pregnancy.

59

In the US about two persons per 1,000 have insulin-dependent diabetes by the age of 20; overall, the insulin-dependent form affects about 150 to 200 persons per 100,000. Non-insulin-dependent diabetes is more common, with as many as 2,000 persons per 100,000 affected.

Symptoms - A physician who suspects diabetes in a patient can often obtain confirmation from testing a sample of urine for its glucose level. Further confirmation is secured when significantly high glucose levels are obtained from blood samples following an overnight fast or from samples taken two hours after a meal. Glucose-tolerance tests are not usually required.

The aims of treatment are to prolong life, relieve symptoms, and prevent long-term complications. Success depends on keeping the level of blood glucose as near normal as possible through maintenance or normal weight, regular physical activity, and careful dietary management.

In people with insulin-dependent diabetes, treatment consists of regular self-injections, one to four times a day, with insulin (either obtained from animals or of a human type synthesized by *genetic engineering*). In addition, the person must follow a diet in which carbohydrate intake is regulated and spread out over the day according to a consistent timetable. In this way, marked fluctuations in the glucose levels in the blood can be avoided.

Disturbances in the careful balance between insulin and glucose intake can result in *hyperglycemia* (too much glucose in the blood), causing the symptoms of the untreated disease, or *hypoglycemia* (too little glucose), which can lead to weakness, confusion, dizziness, sweating, and even unconsciousness and seizures. To help prevent this, diabetics (of both types) are advised to regularly monitor their blood and urine glucose levels with do-it-yourself testing kits.

For difficult-to-control diabetes, an insulin pump is an alternative treatment for those who are willing to monitor their blood glucose levels carefully. Insulin is continuously infused from a refillable pump through a needle implanted in the skin. Control is often no better than that for multiple daily injections.

POT BELLIES

Your spare tire wil not save you from diabetes. If you are sporting a supportive pillow around your bumper rail, your chances are up 50% to developing diabetes after 50 for a man, and 70% for women. There is no mirth in a large girth!

As a precaution against an attack of hypoglycemia, insulin-dependent diabetics need to carry some sugar or glucose with them at all times. Because of the disabling effects of hypoglycemia, insulin-dependent diabetics who drive must declare their disorder to insurance companies and car-licensing authorities. Those with poorly controlled insulin-dependent diabetes are sometimes advised against doing jobs that involve working at a height or operating a public conveyance, and against engaging in activities like race-car driving, or flying, where they may be a danger to themselves and others.

Because the pancreas does produce some insulin in non-insulin-dependent diabetics, the disorder can often be controlled by dietary means alone (regulating the carbohydrate intake with meals spaced out over the day). This not only lowers the blood glucose level, but also reduces weight. If diet fails to lower the glucose level sufficiently, *hypoglycemic* tablets (oral antidiabetic drugs that stimulate the pancreas to produce more insulin) may be prescribed, though these are ineffective unless dietary restrictions are observed.

All people with mild diabetes need regular advice from their physicians so that any complications can be detected and treated at an early stage. Diabetics should wear or carry information identifying them as diabetics in case of an emergency.

Complications eventually develop in a large number of diabetics. These complications tend to be more likely if the diabetes has not been well controlled, but they can occur even if there has been good control. Complications include retinopathy (damage to the retina, the light-sensitive area at the back of the eye, and the blood vessels serving it), peripheral *neu-ropathy* (damage to nerve fibers), and *nephropathy* (kidney damage). Ulcers on the feet, which in severe cases can develop into gangrene, are another risk, but with good foot care they can usually be prevented.

Diabetics also have a higher than average risk of *atherosclerosis* (narrowing of the arteries), *hypertension* (high blood pressure), other *cardiovascular disorders* and *cataracts* (opacities of the lens of the eye).

There are, however, people who have lived full and active lives with diabetes mellitus for 50 years or more with few complications.

With modern treatment and sensible self-monitoring, almost all diabetics can look forward to a normal life. The life expectancy of people who have well-regulated, insulin-dependent diabetes is little difference than that of nondiabetics. Those with the non-insulin-dependent illness have a lightly reduced life expectancy because of circulatory and heart disorders, which often are present when the diabetes is diagnosed.

Magnetic Therapy - In a study of 420 diabetics, 100 were treated using conventional diabetes treatment procedures and 320 were also given additional magnetic therapy.

After one month, the cardiovascular health was checked for both groups. The group with standard procedures had a 28% beneficial effectiveness for their circulatory health while the group that had additional magnetic therapy had a significant 74% increase in blood flow through their cardiovascular system which is extremely important for diabetics faced with amputations of their lower appendages. [46]

In another research of 72 diabetics with purulent (infected-pus filled) wounds of their legs, all 72 were

46. Kirillovan, I.B., et al., *Magnetic Therapy in Comprehensive Treatment of Vascular Complications of Diabetics*, Klin Med, Moscow, 1996

treated with magnetic therapy to increase blood flow in addition to standard, conservative medical procedures. All were safe from imminent amputation. [47]

Dr. Michael I. Weintraub, a professor of neurology at New York Medical College, as reported in Family Circle, did a research study of magnetic therapy with diabetic patients suffering from painful neuropathy. A remarkable 75% of the patients using magnetic therapy with conventional procedures had a positive reversal of symptoms. The control group without magnetic therapy showed a 50% reduction. [48]

47. Kuliev, R.A., et al., *Magnetic Therapy used in Combined Treatment of Suppurative Wounds in Diabetes*, Vestos Khir Im., Russia, 1992
48. Weintraub, Michael K., *Diabetic Pain with Use of Magnetic Therapy*, American Journal of Pain Management, January 1998

EARACHES

Description - As a child, nothing hurts more than a throbbing earache (otitis media). Inflammation of the middle ear (the cavity between the eardrum and the inner ear).

Causes - The inflammation occurs as the result of an upper respiratory tract infection (such as a cold) extending up the eustachian tube, the passage that connects the back of the nose to the middle ear. The tube may become blocked by the inflammation or sometimes by enlarged *adenoids*, which are often associated with

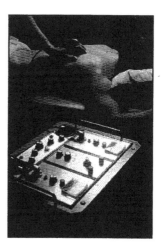

infections of the nose and throat. As a result, fluid produced by the inflammation - along with pus in bacterial infections - is not drained off through the tube but accumulates in the middle ear.

The chronic phase of otitis media follows an upper respiratory infection that has produced acute otitis media.

Children are particularly susceptible to otitis media, probably because of the shortness of their eustachian tubes. About one in six children suffer from the acute form in the first year of life and about one in 10 in each of the next six years. Some children have recurrent attacks. Chronic otitis media is much less common because, in most cases, attacks of acute middle ear infection clear with treatment.

Symptoms - Acute otitis media is marked by sudden, severe earache, a feeling of fullness in the ear, deafness, tinnitus (ringing or buzzing in the ear), and fever. Sometimes the eardrum burst, relieving the pain and resulting in a discharge of pus. In this case, healing usually occurs in several days.

FUN FACT MEDICAL HISTORY

In chronic otitis media, pus constantly exudes from a perforation in the eardrum and there is some degree of deafness. Complications of the condition include *otitis external* (inflammation of the outer ear; damage to the bones in the middle ear, causing more deafness (sometimes total) in the affected ear; or a *cholesteatoma* (a matted ball of sometimes infected skin debris). In rare cases, infection spreads inward from an infected ear, causing *mastoiditis* or a *brain abscess*.

In the 1930's, during the famous "Long March," Mao Tse-túng's Red Army had malaria (Latin: mal-bad, aria-air), Having no drugs, the malaria was beaten using only acupuncture.

The Timetables of History

Magnetic Therapy - Magnetic therapy was used on patients with hearing problems. The use of magnetic therapy was used to increase blood flow to the ear area. This increased cellular oxidation of the otitis perimeter stimulated greater ability to amplify both high and low sound waves; thus, 100% of the subjects reported much greater hearing capabilities. Unfortunately, after the magnetic therapy was stopped, the subjects were tested again and 75% had lost some hearing benefits because they were no longer using the magnetic therapy. The magnetic therapy was then reintroduced to this group and

80% when again tested showed improvement. It appears from the testing and retesting that these patients will only have continued good hearing while they continue to use the magnetic therapy. [49]

In a Moscow children's hospital, 52 children over a two year study period, who had earaches due to a bacterial infection rising up through the eustachian tubes were all treated with magnetic therapy and 98% had a shortness of the duration of the pain and suffering. [50]

In 1954, Dr. Linus Pauling won the Nobel Prize in part for his research on magnetic therapy and its efficient application of reducing infections and inflammations by increasing the oxidation to the inflicted area with up to a 300% increase of blood flow with oxygen to the painful area. Ear infections are nothing to fool with for they can lead to total deafness and in rare cases brain swelling which can kill you. Use magnetic therapy on the next ear infection of your loved ones.

Simple tips for healthier ears:
❑ Don't insert any object into your ear canal.
❑ Avoid forceful nose blowing.
❑ Stay away from extremely loud noises, music and firearms.
❑ Wear earplugs when your ears are exposed to water sports and swimming.
❑ If you think that there is a live insect in your ear, don't try to lure it out with a bright light. This can make it crawl deeper into the ear.
❑ If something solid gets down into the ear canal, don't us oil or water, It can cause the foreign body to go deeper or cause the ear to swell.
Medical Sources
Taber's Cyclopedic Medical Dictionary, Edition 16, F.A. Davis Co., Philadelphia, 1989.
The Merck Manual, Sixteenth Edition, Merck Research Laboratories, Rahway, NJ, 1992

49. Sunstov, V.V., *Treatment of Acute Diffuse Hearing Loss with Magnetic Therapy*, Vestn Otorinolaringol, USSR, 1993
50. Sunstov, V.V., *Treatment of Oitits Media with Magnetic Therapy*, Vestn Otorinolaringol, USSR, 1996

EPILEPSY

Description - A tendency to recurrent seizures or temporary alteration in one or more brain functions.

Seizures are defined as transient neurological abnormalities caused by abnormal electrical activity in the brain. Human activities, thoughts, perceptions and emotions are normally the result of the regulated and orderly electrical excitation of nerve cells in the brain. During a seizure, a chaotic and unregulated electrical discharge occur. In some cases a stimulus such as a flashing light sets off this abnormal sequence, but often seizures appear spontaneously.

Causes - Seizures are a symptom of brain dysfunction and, like symptoms in other parts of the body, can result from a wide variety of disease or injury. Seizures may occur in association with *head injury*, birth trauma, brain infection (such as *meningitis* or *encephalitis*), *brain tumor, stroke,* drug intoxication, drug or alcohol withdrawal states, or metabolic imbalance in the body. A tendency to seizures may develop for no obvious reason or there may be an inherited predisposition.

About one person in 200 suffers from epilepsy. The number of epileptics in the US is estimated to be close to 1 million. The disorder usually starts in childhood or adolescence. Many people outgrow epilepsy and do not require medication.

Symptoms - epileptic seizures can be classified into

two broad groups - generalized and partial seizures. The form a seizure takes depends on the part of the brain in which it arises and on how widely and rapidly it fans out from its point of origin. Generalized siezures, which cause loss of consciousness, affect the whole body and may arise over a wide area of the brain. Temporal lobe

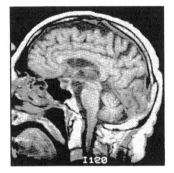

epilepsy is a type of partial seizure. Partial seizures, in which consciousness may be retained, are usually caused by damage to a more limited area of the brain. Though partial seizures begin in a limited area, the electrical disturbance may spread and affect the whole brain, causing a generalized seizure.

Many people with epilepsy lead normal lives and have no symptoms between seizures. Some can tell when an attack is imminent by experiencing an aura (a restless, irritable, or uncomfortable feeling).

In making the diagnosis, the physician seeks as much information as possible about the attacks. Since patients frequently do not have recall, information may be obtained from witnesses. After a complete neurological examination, the physician usually orders an EEG (EEG and ECG determine brain waves and heart waves and record them on graph paper for diagnosis. Both are only possible by the utilization of magnetism) to help with the diagnosis. It is important to realize that the EEG cannot always absolutely confirm or refute the diagnosis of seizures, and that the results must be weighed in light of other clinical findings. Sometimes tests of heart function (such as an *ECG* or *Holter monitor*) are obtained to exclude cardiac irregularities as a cause of loss of consciousness in an adult. Patients thought to have seizures are usually given *CT scanning* of the brain and *blood tests* to check for the conditions associated with epilepsy. Opinion is divided on whether a single seizure should be treated; physicians agree that people with recurrent seizures should take *anticonvulsant drugs*.

HOLISTIC CURE
Epileptic seizures are treated by massive amounts of prescription drugs in America. However, there is now a proven holistic method to help epileptics without drugs or surgery. Many seizures are started by flushing, flickering or strong lights from the electromagnetic spectrum. It has recently been found and proven effective to wear blue (only blue) sunglasses to stop seizures. The blue filters the wavelengths so the brain waves do not trigger a seizure. Found to be extremely effective.
Journal of Epilepsia
(33,3:517)

Magnetic Therapy - A form of magnetic therapy is call TMS (transcranial magnetic stimulation) and it has been found to have dramatic results on epileptics. In Gottingen, Germany, a 1999 research studied 5 women and 4 men (21 to 40 years old) who suffered severe epilepsy on a daily basis from partial to *gran mal* seizures. Of the nine, one reported no change with the magnetic therapy, two reported a lessening of the severity, but still had the same amount of weekly attacks, one showed a decrease of 20%, two showed a decrease of 20% to 50% and three showed a decrease of more than 50%. For epileptics this is a dramatic decrease, because fully 25% of all epileptics show no results to drug therapy and the strong drugs they use are detrimental for the patient's overall health. Here, using magnetic therapy we have an 88% positive result with no drug side effects. However, eight weeks after the nine patients stopped using the magnetic therapy, everyone returned to their old patterns of frequency and severity. Therefore, in order to be effective, the epileptic patients will have to stay on magnetic therapy for the rest of their lives. [51]

In another study, four severe adult epileptics experienced reduced seizures with the use of magnetic therapy by changing their biorhythms through the synchronization of the body's natural circadian periods (our bodies all have a natural flow like the tides of the oceans, when these healthy ebbs are interfered with by epileptic seizure or other problems, we become unbalanced and suffer illnesses.) [52]

Another research on severe epileptics found that magnetic therapy lessened behavioral disturbances and seizure frequency in teenagers experiencing sexual changes. [53]

51. Tergan, F., etal., *TMS Improves Intractable Epilepsy*, Lancet 353:2209, UK, 1999
52. P.A. Anninos, et al., *Magnetic Field Therapy Alters the Circadian Periods of Seizures*, Internation Journal of Neuro Sci, April 1992
53. Sandyk, r., etal., *Attenuation of Epilepsy with Application of Magnetic Therapy*, International Journal of Neuro Sci, Sept. 1992

FRACTURES

Description - A break in a bone, most commonly caused by a fall. A bone is usually broken directly across its width, but can also be fractured lengthwise, obliquely or spirally.

The types of fractures are divided into two main types: closed (or simple) and open (or compound). In a closed fracture the broken bone ends remain beneath the skin and little or no surrounding tissues are damaged, in an open fracture one or both bone ends project through the skin.

Fractures may also be classified according to the shape or pattern of the break (see box).

If the two bone ends have moved apart the fracture is termed displaced; in an undisplaced fracture the ends remain in alignment and there is simply a crack to the bone.

Causes - Most fractures are caused by a sudden injury that exerts more force on the bone that it can withstand. The force may be direct, as when a finger is hit by a hammer, or indirect as when twisting the foot exerts severe stress on the tibia (shin).

Some diseases, such as *osteoporosis* and certain forms of cancer, weaken bone so much that it takes only a minor injury - or none at all - for the bone to break. This type of fracture is termed pathological.

Common sites of fracture include the hand, the wrist *(see Colles' fracture)*, the ankle joint, the clavicle (collarbone), and the neck of the *femur* (thigh bone), usually as the result of a fall.

Elderly people are the most prone to fractures because they fall more and because their bones are fragile.

Symptoms - There is usually swelling and tenderness at the site of the fracture and, in some cases, deformity or projecting bone ends. The pain is often severe and is usually made worse by any movement of the area.

Magnetic Therapy - Orthopedic surgeon Dr. Richard Rogachefsky, of the University of Miami School of Medicine has done much research on bone fracture repairs using permanent magnets with remarkable results. One particular difficult case involved a man with a gunshot wound to the hand which fractured the thumb. The magnet was placed in the cast over the broken thumb. Usually a complicated fracture in a continuously active body area like the hand would take approximately 2 months to knit properly. Through the use of magnetic therapy, the man's hand was stabilized and useful in only 6 weeks, because magnets were used to accelerate the healing process. [54]

The Federal Food & Drug Administration (FDA) which evaluates all the medical information for efficacy and safety for all medications, medical procedures and devices has appoved in 1978 magnetic therapy for the

54. Rogachefsky, R., *Use of Tectonis Magnet for Treatment of Hand After Gunshop,* North American Academy of Magnetic Therapy Newsletter, Miami, FL, 1997

healing of bone fractures and it is approved by Medicare, Medicaid, HMO's and all insurance carriers as an approved medical procedure. [55]

Dr. Zachary Friedenberg, of the University of Pennsylvania was in 1971 one of the first orthopedic surgeons in America to successfully use magnetic therapy to cure bone fractures. Today, more than 80% of America's *"bone doctors"* use magnetic therapy to knit fractures with a success rate of 75-80%; especially as a treatment for the difficult *nonunion* fractures, fusion failures and pseudoarthrosis. [56]

LOW SALT
Post-menopausal women should be on low-salt diet because table salt leaches away calcium from the body. Calcium depletion from salt is a major contributing factor to osteoporosis.
Archives of Internal Medicine (151,4:757

There has been a lot of American research done on the positive effects of using magnetic therapy to help bone fractures heal. The basic, scientific reason why it works is that magnetism moves calcium ions into the bone mass. Everybody needs calcium for a healthy lifestyle, but it is the location of these calcium ions in your body that determines your degree of health. Calcium in your joints produces arthritis and calcium in your cardiovascular system produces atherosclerosis which leads to high blood pressure, clots, strokes and heart attacks. Magnetic therapy simply moves these random, free-flowing calcium ions out of these undesirable locations and attaches them to your bone mass, stopping the onset of crippling osteoporosis. In fractures, magnetism

55. Lawrence, R., et al., *Magnet Therapy - the Pain Cure Alternative,* Prima Health Publications, Rocklin, CA, 1998
56. Bassett, C.A., *A noninvasive Therapeutic Modality for Fracture Nonunion*, Orthopedic Review 15:12, 1986

bridges the gap with calcium so the bone will knit faster and better. Dr. K.M. Hansen proved how this worked in a 1938 study in Scandanavia. [57]

In 1993, Kenneth Miner and Richard Markoll worked with osteroarthritis patients and magnetic therapy and these subjects showed improvements in 6 clinical variables ranging from 23% - 63%. The control group using a nonmagnetic placebo device had improvements of only 2%-18%. [58]

Get the Right Calcium
Calcium supplements at $200MM per year are the #2 after Vit. C in over-the-counter sales. First, only buy Citrate form and not the Carbonate form. Although more expensive, your body absorbs much more. Second, take it with Vit. D for greater benefits.
U.S. Pharmacist

At the Creighton University School of Medicine in Omaha, Nebraska, clinical research was done on rats and sheep to prove the effectiveness of magnetic therapy on strengthening the bones from the effects of osteoporosis. A clinical trial was subsequently performed on 52 people suffering bone loss, and the positive results were registered. [59]

Other supportive studies on the remarkable ability of magnetic therapy to heal bone fractures are:

In the *Journal of Bone Joint Surgery*, one study showed that 38 patients with ununited, wide-gap frac-

57. Hausen, K.M., *Influence of Magnetism Upnn the Human Organism*, Acta Med Scan, 1938
58. Owen, L., *Pain free with Magnetic Therapy*, Prima Publishing, Roseville, CA, 2000
59. Trock, D.H., et al., *Magnet Therapy in the Treatment of Osteoarthritis*, Journal of Rheumatology, 1994

tures, synovial pseudoarthritis and malaligument had an outstanding 93% recovery rate. Most of these patients were given up on as having unhealable fractures. [60] Another 125 patients with ununited fractures and tibial diaphysis were 87% healed by use of magnetic therapy. [61] Another study found through the use of magnetic therapy, 35 of 44 non-united scaphoid fractures which resisted treatment for 6 months, healed in 4.3 months using magnets. [62] In a landmark, FDA approved clinical study at Columbia Presbyterian Hospital in New York City, 1077 fracture patients were treated with magnetic therapy and an amazing 81% had a successful completion of healing bone fractures. [63]

I could bury you with hundreds of medically reviewed studies on the ability of magnets to help bones heal. This fracture procedure is accepted worldwide as a bona fide addition to conventional bone setting and cast immobilization to heal broken bones. It is amazing however, that many American doctors still do not use this easy, inexpensive way to help their patients recover from broken bones.

60. Bassett, C.S., et al., *Treatment of Thrapeutically Resistant Non-unions Using Magnetic Therapy,* Journal of Bone Joint Surgery, 1982
61. Meskens, M.W., et al., *Treatment of Delayed Union of the Tibia,* Bulletin Hospital Joint Disease Orthop. Inst., Fall 1988
62. Drykman, G.K., et al., *Treatment of Nonunited Seapoid Fractures with Magnet Therapy and Cast,* Journal of Hand Surgery, May 1986
63. Bassett, C.A., et al., *Magnetic Therapy in Ununited Fractures and Failed Arthrodeses,* JAMA 247(5) , February 5, 1982

HEADACHES

Description - One of the most common types of pain; a headache is very rarely a sign of some underlying, serious disorder. The pain of a headache comes from outside the brain (the brain tissue itself does not contain sensory nerves). Pain arises from the meninges (the outer linings of the brain) and from the scalp and its blood vessels and muscles. It is produced by tension in, or stretching of, these structures.

The pain may be felt all over the head or may occur in one part only - for example, in the back of the neck, the forehead, or one side of the head. Sometimes the pain  moves to another part of the head during the course of the headache. The pain may be superficial or deep, throbbing or sharp, and there may be accompanying or preliminary symptoms, such as nausea, vomiting, and visual or sensory disturbances. Many headaches are simply the body's response to some adverse stimulus, such as hunger or a change in the weather. These headaches usually clear up in a few hours and leave no aftereffects.

Tension headaches, caused by tightening in the muscles of the face, neck and scalp as a result of stress or poor posture, are also common. They may last for days or weeks and can cause variable degrees of discomfort.

Some types of headaches are especially painful and persistent, but, despite these symptoms, do not indicate any progressive disorder. *Migraine* is a severe, incapacitating headache preceded or accompanied by visual and/or stomach disturbances. Cluster headaches cause intense pain behind one eye and may wake the sufferer nightly for periods of weeks or months.

Causes - Common causes of headache include hangover, irregular meals, prolonged travel, poor posture, a noisy or stuffy work environment, excitement and excessive sleep. Recent research has shown that certain foods (such as cheese, chocolate and red wine) trigger migraine attacks in susceptible people. *Food additives* may also cause headaches. Other causes include *sinusitis,* toothache, ear infection, head injury, and *cervical osteoarthritis.* (See also chart, overleaf.)

Types of Headaches
1. Tension
2. Migraine
3. Sinus
4. Hunger
5. Heat
6. Drug
7. Cluster
8. Hypertension

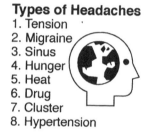

Among the rare causes of headaches are *brain tumor, hypertension* (high blood pressure), *temporal arteritis* (inflammation of the arteries of the brain and scalp), *aneurysm* (localized swelling of blood vessel), and increased pressure within the skull.

WHY ME?
Migraine headaches can be especially debilitating and are caused by vascular contractions. Medical science does not know why, but 70% of migraine sufferers are female.
Dr. Patricia Solbach
Menninger Clinic

Magnetic Therapy - Simple, tension headaches are the easiest for magnetism to work by bringing cellular oxygen to the brain and stimulating the flow of endorphins, most of these common headaches go away quickly. [64] In America, 40

64. Coghill, Roger, *The Book of Magnet Healing - A Holistic Approach to Pain Relief,* Simon & Schuster, London, UK, 2000

million of us have at least one headache that will require medical attention. About 75% of Americans have a significant headache annually. Surprisingly, one of the greatest causes of headache pain is the result of taking prescription pharmaceuticals. The greatest occurrence of drug side effects are headaches. [65] The second greatest cause of headaches in America is cigarette smoking and alcohol consumption; especially, when taken together. [66] In a British study of 34,000 overweight people, and a similar study of obese Americans, found that people who are fat suffer greater pain from headaches because of the psychological stress on their bodies; especially their extended midriffs pulling on their lower back muscles and psychologically because chubby people feel rejected in our slim and trim world of desirability and suffer low self-esteem which cause down in the dumps headache patterns. [67] Many foods also cause headaches in some people. High on the list are seasonings (sodium nitrates, monosodium glutamate - MSG), tyramine found in chocolate, aged cheeses and red wine, artificial sweeteners, yogurt, dried fruit, buttermilk, beans, pickled and marinated food. All of these cause headaches in some people, but magnetic therapy exposure will also reduce the headache causing effects through better circulation (get rid of the toxins faster) and cellular oxidation (burn up the pesky pesticides). [68]

65. Mauskip, A., et al., *A Practical Approach to Pain Management*, Little, Brown, Inc., Boston, MA, 1996
66. Pilowsky, I., *Abnormal Illness Behavior*, British Journal of Medical Psychology, London, UK, 1969
67. Eisendrath, S.J., *Psychiatric Aspects of Chronic Pain*, Neurology, London, UK, 1995
68. Markenson, J.A., *Mechanism of Chronic Pain*, American Journal of Medicine, July 31, 1996.

Stress is a major cause of headaches and many people today combat this product of our rat race existence by the application of magnetic therapy which has proved remarkably effective in reducing everyday stress and hypertension. [69] According to Ron Lawrence, M.D., Ph.D., many headaches are the results of hypoxia (oxygen starvation). He states that magnetic therapy helps to unclog arteries so that oxygenized blood rapidly comes to the infected area relieving the headache pain.[70]

Acute migraine headache sufferers have successful results from the pain by using magnetic therapy. [71] In an extensive study conducted in Hungary, a group of chronic headache sufferers were treated with Magnetic Therapy. The results indicated that 88% of the tension sufferers had good results, migraine sufferers had a 60% success

MEDICAL ALERT
When Headaches Can Mean Real Trouble

"The average person" says Seymour Diamond, M.D., "typically has a tension headache." No big deal, no danger. But occasionally headaches are warning symptoms for serious disease. Here are the red flags.
• You are over 40 and never had recurring headaches before.
• The headaches have changed locations.
• The headaches are getting stronger.
• The headaches are coming more frequently.
• The headaches do not fit a recognizable pattern; that is, there seems to be nothing in particular that triggers them.
• Headaches have begun to disrupt your life; you've missed work on several occasions.
• The headaches are accompanied by neurological symptoms, such as numbness, dizziness, blurred vision, or memory loss.
• The headaches coincide with other medical problems or pain.
If you experience these symptoms, see your doctor.

69. Birla, G.S., et al., *Magnet Therapy*, Healing Arts Press, Rochester,t Vermont 1999
70. Lawrence, Ron, et al., *Magnet Therapy, the Pain Cure Alternative*, Prima Health, Rocklin, CA, 1998
71. Sandyk, R., *The Influence of Magnets on Migraine and Cluster Headaches*, International Journal of NeuroSci, Nov-Dec, 1992

rate, cervical migraine sufferers had a 69% success, and psychogenic headache patients had a 60% reduction in frequency and pain. [72]

Finally, in a cutting edge program to prove the effectiveness of magnetic therapy's ability to ease pain by increasing blood circulation and stimulation of the body's production of natural endorphins, two groups of 100 participants each of chronic headache sufferers were tested. The first group received standard, nonnarcotic, acetaminophen analgesic medication (Tylenol, an over-the-counter drug). The second group received Tylenol plus magnetic therapy. After seven days, the first group on Tylenol was taken off the pills and then tested after seven days with no medication. Only 23% after two weeks said that their headaches went away. The other group on magnetic therapy for one week on, one week off, had a 66% loss of headache pain. Thus, it appears obvious that the magnetic therapy works better than just Tylenol alone. Plus, there are no side effects with magnetism while Tylenol has a potential of liver damage over extended use.

Are you tired of headaches? Maybe it is time for you to try a natural alternative in magnetic therapy.[73]

72. Prusinski, A., et al., *Magnetic Therapy in the Therapy of a Headache*, Hungarian Symposium on Magnetogherapy, Szekesfehervar, Hungary, 1987
73. Lazar, L., et al., *Magnet Therapy in the Treatment of Headache Symptoms*, Journal of Bioelectricity, 1998.

INFECTIONS, INFLAMMATIONS AND WOUNDS

Description - Infection - The establishment of a colony of disease-causing microorganisms (such as bacteria, viruses, or fungi) in the body. The organisms actively reproduce and cause disease directly by damage to cells or indirectly by toxins they release. Infection normally provokes a response from the *immune system,* which accounts for many of the features of the infection.

Toxic symptoms, such as fever, weakness, and joint aches, are expressions of *infectious disease.* In such cases, the microorganisms are often spread throughout the body (this is called "systemic" infection). Infection may also be localized within a particular tissue or area, often through spread of organisms from parts of the body where they are harmless to parts where they are harmful (e.g., through leakage from the intestines into the abdomen to cause *peritonitis*).

Entry of microorganisms from soil into wounds or during the course of surgical operations and procedures is another common cause of localized infection. In the early days of surgery, infection of internal body cavities was the major (and frequently fatal) risk to the patient. Antiseptic surgical techniques have largely eliminated this problem.

Localized infections (as opposed to infectious diseases) can be avoided by standard hygienic measures, such as keeping the hands clean, not picking at blemishes, washing and covering cuts and grazes, having wounds attended to by a physician, and seeking regular dental

82

treatment.

Symptoms - Localized infection is generally followed by inflammation, which increases the flow of blood to the infected area, bringing white blood cells and other components of the immune system. Symptoms and signs usually include pain, redness, swelling, formation of a pus-filled abscess at the site of infection, and sometimes a rise in temperature.

Description - Inflammation
Redness, swelling, heat and pain in a tissue due to chemical or physical injury, or to infection.

When body tissues are damaged, specialized *mast cells* release a chemical called *histamine* (other substances are also involved in the inflammatory response, but histamine is believed to be responsible for most of the effects). Histamine increases blood flow to the damaged tissue, which causes the redness and heat. It also makes the blood capillaries more leaky, resulting in fluid oozing out of them and into the tissues, which causes localized swelling. The pain of inflammation is due to stimulation of nerve endings by the inflammatory chemicals.

SPORTS STARS
More and more athletes are using the natural health alternative of magnetic therapy over drugs. Today's jocks are a lot smarter and earn a lot more money than players of yesterday. They are informed and want to extend their careers as long as possible. This is the reason magnetic therapy is so popular.

Symptoms - Inflammation is usually accompanied by an accumulation of white blood cells, which are attracted by the inflammatory chemicals. These white cells help destroy invading microorganisms and are involved in repairing the damaged tissue. Thus, inflammation is an essential part of the body's response to injury and infection.

If inflammation is inappropriate (as in *rheumatoid arthritis* and other *autoimmune disorders*), it may be suppressed by *corticosteroid drugs*.

Description - Wounds - Any damage to the skin and/or underlying tissues caused by an accident, act of violence, or surgery. Wounds in which the skin or mucous membrane are broken are called open; those in which they remain intact are termed closed.

Types - Wounds can be divided into the following broad categories - an incised wound (an injury in which the skin is cleanly cut, or a surgical incision); an abrasion (a graze in which surface tissue is scraped away); a laceration (a wound in which the skin is torn, such as an animal or human bite); a penetrating wound (such as a stab or gunshot wound); and a contusion (a wound in which the underlying tissues are damaged by a blunt instrument). This type of soft tissue injury may include damage to subcutaneous tissue, muscle, bone, blood vessels, and/or nerves. When the wound lies over the thorax or abdomen, internal organs may also be bruised or more

ZAP IT!
Here's a mystery. Routinely, one particular office worker goes out to get lunch for the others. One day she gets very sick from Hepatitis-A infection from the take out food. Why only her? Well, she ate her lunch on the way back to the office, while the others microwaved theirs to warm it up. Microwaves kill most infection causing bacteria.
George McDermott
Millennium Age.

severely damaged. Considerable bleeding can occur with little outward evidence.

Many penetrating wounds and some contused wounds are deceptive in appearance, showing little external sign of damage but involving serious internal injury. Low-velocity gunshot injuries cause tissue damage all along the path of the projectile. High-velocity gunshot injuries may also damage distant structures as a result of shock waves traveling through tissues. In stab wounds, vital organs may be perforated or major blood vessels severed. In contusions, the liver, spleen, or kidney may be ruptured and cause internal bleeding.

Catfish Caution
All fish carry bacteria unfriendly to humans, but catfish are real bad. Their scales and fins have special germs which can easily cause bone infections (osteomyelitis) which can quickly cause severe inflammation resolved by amputation. Don't handle live catfish unless you want to lose a finger!
Emergency Med.
(24,4:195)

Magnetic Therapy - A 38 year-old woman suffered from chronic vaginal infections. After six months of sleeping on a magentized sleep system, she no longer had reoccurrences. [74] Another woman suffered from Guillain-Barre syndrome which is a viral infection of the nervous system which robs you of your mobility. Unable to walk or even raise her arms, after two days she was 70% mobile. [75]

In an extensive Italian study was done of 3,014 patients suffering from joint inflammation. The doctors used magnetic therapy to reduce pain and restore joint

74. Birla, G.S., et al., *Magnet Therapy*, Healing Arts Press, Rochester, VT, 1999
75. Ibid

mobility. The positive rating of 7.8% is an outstanding result and illustrates the powerful benefits of applying magnets to swollen, inflamed joints.[76]

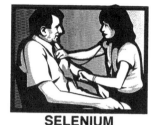

SELENIUM

As people age they become more susceptible to infections because their immune systems are compromised. To boost your immunology, take the mineral selenium. This dietary supplement is inexpensive and works wonders.

Amer. Journal of Clinical Nutrition (53,5:1323)

Bringing oxygen to the inflammation site is a common application in fighting low-grade infections. You can do this a number of ways. Ice works fine, as does a heating pad, or an ointment like BenGay, but nothing does it better, cleaner and safer than magnetic therapy.[77]

For wound healing, Dr. D. Man, a plastic surgeon of Boca Raton, Florida, has used magnetic therapy on post-operative patients to accelerate their wound healing; especially, after liposuction surgeries. The results have been outstanding with the discoloration scar tissue and incision marks disappearing in half the time of conventional convalescence.[78]

In a British study, a doctor found tremendous relief from soft-tissue injuries and inflammations from sport injuries.[79] Dan Marino, former Miami Dolphins quarterback was to be sidelined with torn tendons and painfully

76. Sanseverino, E.R., et al., *Therapeutic Effects of Magnetic Therapy on Joint Diseases*, Panminerva Med, Italy, 1992
77. Whitaker, Julian - *The Pain Relief Breakthrough*, Little, Brown & Co., Boston, MA 1998
78. Man, D., *The Influence of Magnetic Therapy on Wound Healing*, Journal of Plastic and Reconstuctive Surgery, Dec. 1999
79. Coats, G.C., *Magnetic Therapy on Soft-Tissue Injuries*, British Journal of Sports Medicine, UK, 1989

swollen ankle for 8 weeks, but his trainer, Ryan Vermillion, used magnetic therapy and Dan was back playing in just 3 weeks. Denver Broncos All-Star linebacker, Bill Romanowski sleeps every night on a magnetized sleep system and credits his football longevity on magnetic therapy. Henry Ellard of the Redskins and Chris Jones of the baseball San Diego Padres use magnets for pulled muscles. Lately, most teams are putting magnetized pads on the team bench to allow the players to overcome soreness from the game. Over 75% of sports stars in football, baseball, basketball, Olympics, tennis, golf, hockey, rodeo, etc. use magnetic therapy to lower the incidence of infections, inflammation and wounds.[80]

It only makes sense to use the natural alternative of magnetic therapy to relieve your personal pain and suffering from infections, inflammation and wounds.

Contaminated Makeup
Your makeup is one of the greatest sources of infections and inflammations.
1. Throw out old makeup if it becomes hard, odorous or changes color.
2. Keep tightly closed.
3. Never share makeup.
4. Keep out of sunlight.
5. Don't get in your eyes.
6. Use only as directed.
7. Be careful of cold sores.
FDA Consumer (25,9:19)

80. Lawrence, Ron, et al., *Magnet Therapy, the Pain Cure Alternative*, Prime Health, Rocklin, CA, 1998

INSOMNIA

Description - Trouble sleeping. Insomnia is a common problem. A national survey has shown that one in every three US adults has some trouble sleeping and that hypnotic drugs are among the most widely used of all medicines. People with insomnia have difficulty falling asleep or staying asleep. Most insomnia sufferers also complain of increased daytime fatigue, irritability, and difficulty coping.

Animal Infections
All animals have bacteria that can infect humans. Cats have Pasteurella multocida which infects and inflames more humans that any other. Animal bites can cause tetanus (lockjaw). Be very careful, get a tetanus shot.
Emergency Medicine
(24,4:195)

Causes - The most common cause of insomnia is worry about a problem (such as bad news received during the day or a difficult task to cope with the following morning), but other causes are implicated in about half of all cases.

Causes include physical disorders such as *sleep apnea* (a breathing problem), *restless legs*, environmental factors (such as noise and light), lifestyle factors (such as too much coffee in the evening, lack of exercise during the day, or keeping erratic hours), or misuse of hypnotic drugs (*see Antianxiety drugs; Barbiturate drugs*).

Insomnia also can be a symptom of a psychiatric illness. People with *anxiety* and/or *depression* may have difficulty getting to sleep; those suffering from depression typically wake early in the morning, sleeping much less

88

than usual is common in *mania,* in which the person is so full of drive and energy that he or she does not need much sleep. *Schizophrenia* often causes people to pace at night, aroused by "voices" or delusions. People with *dementia* or other brain disorders may be afraid in the dark and become restless and noisy, confused by the shadows and sounds of the night.

Withdrawal syndrome from hypnotic drugs, antidepressants, tranquilizers, and illicit drugs (such as heroin) may cause many weeks of insomnia.

People sometimes believe they have insomnia because of misconception about the amount of sleep they need. In fact, sleep needs vary greatly, with some people requiring less than four hours and others needing more than 10. Some people who think they have insomnia are in fact "out of phase," lying awake for hours after going to bed, but sleeping normally if allowed to sleep late in the morning.

Symptoms - If there is an obvious physical or physiological cause for insomnia, it is treated. For long-term insomnia with no obvious cause, *EEG* recordings of brain-wave patterns and an assessment of breathing, muscle activity, and other bodily functions during sleep may be useful in discovering the extent and pattern of the problem. Keeping a log of sleep patterns may also be helpful.

Studies have shown that many insomniacs sleep much more than they think they do. However, they also tend to wake more frequently than normal sleepers. It is the quality, more than the quantity, of sleep that is the problem in insomnia. People with insomnia should ensure they are active during the day and should establish a regular time and routine for going to bed each night and a regular time for waking in the morning. *Sleeping drug* should be used only with a physician's advice.

Magnetic Therapy - Insomnia is associated with low levels of the neurotransmitter serotonin. Magnetic therapy's unique effect on the body is that it stimulates the natural secretion of both serotonin and endorphin levels in the body. Both are calming, sleep inducing, 100% natural bodily chemicals that help you sleep naturally with no drug side effects. [81]

THE DOZING DOZEN SLEEP TIPS
1. Keep a regular sleep schedule.
2. Avoid alcohol, caffeine and nicotine.
3. Don't eat "heavy" before sleep.
4. Wind down before going to bed.
5. Have a comfortable mattress.
6. Sleep in a dark, quiet room
7. Get regular, daily exercise.
8. Don't take naps after 2 p.m.
9. Leave your problems behind.
10. Don't toss & turn, read a book.
11. Watch your prescription drugs.
12. Take lowest dose sleeping pills.
American Family Physician
(45,3: 1262

In Japan, which is rated number one in the world by the World Health Organization (WHO part of the UN) for health and longevity, [82] has 30 million households going to sleep each night on a magnetized sleep system. The Japanese lead the world in overall health, longevity and robust years (robust years are the life span where a person is mobile and free to do the activities they enjoy without assisted living, nursing care or confinement).

81. Whitaker, Julian, et al., *The Pain Relief Breakthrough - the Power of Magnets*, Little, Brown & Co., Boston, MA, 1998
82. Lowe, Carl, *World Health Report*, Energy Times, Long Beach, CA, March 2001

Of the 24 industrialized nations, America ranks last in health, longevity and robust years. However, from the end of robust years until death, we are number one because our medical system is the greatest at keeping us alive under assisted, nursing and hospital conditions. The average American will live 6 years from the time they lose their independence until death finally intervenes. Of course, this comes at a very high emotional price and financially, the average American will spend 75% of their life savings, plus family money in the last 3 years of life just to barely stay alive. But, the good, old USA is #1 in nursing homes.

POPULAR PROBLEM
About 205 of Americans have problems falling asleep at night, and 40% have trouble falling back to sleep if they are awakened. The biggest reason is stress from life's problems. Try to train your mind to give them up to a Higher Power when you hit the sheets.
Southern Medical Journal
(84,3:1268)

In Tokyo Communications Hospital, Dr. Kazuo Shimoda did a research study on 431 patients with insomnia.

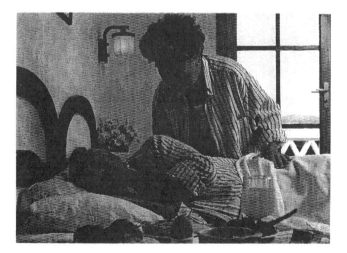

After one week of sleeping on a magnetized mattress pad 97.47% said they were sleeping soundly.[83]

According to Dr. Gary Null, emcee of the very popular PBS health show, *The Gary Null Show*, states in his book *Healing with Magnets*, that magnetic therapy stimulates the pineal gland in the brain's limbic system to secrete natural melatonin which calms the body and induces restful sleep. It is time for you to use magnets as a natural alternative so you can get a wonderful night's sleep and have plenty of energy tomorrow. [84]

SLEEP vs. DRUGS

The second biggest cause of insomnia is prescription drug side effects. Triazolan, a popular sleep pill, has caused some alarming secondary reactions such as mental instability, memory impairment and amnesia. A 33 year old man took Naproxen for shoulder pain an went through hellish nightmares until he stopped. Below are drug you should never take before sleep.

- Naproxen • Doxepin • Fluphenazine
- Diphenhydramine • Beta Blockers
- Reserpine • Thioridazine
- Thiothixene • Buspirone • Verapamil

The People's Pharmacy

83. Shimodair, K., *Magnetic Therapy and Insomnia*, Tokyo Communications Hospitall, Tokyo, Japan, 1990
84. Null, Gary, et al., *Healing with Magnets*, Carroll & Graf Publishers, Inc., N.Y.C., NY, 1998

KIDNEY DISORDERS

Description - The organ responsible for filtering the blood and excreting waste products and excess water in the form of urine. The kidney, ureter, bladder and urethra make up the *urinary tract.*

There are two kidneys, each about 4 to 5 inches long and about 6 ounces in weight. They lie in the abdomen underneath the liver on the right and the spleen on the left. The arteries that supply the kidneys arise directly from the aorta (the main artery of the body leading from the heart). Once within the kidneys, the renal arteries divide into smaller and smaller branches, ending in capillaries in the glomeruli (the kidney's primary filtering units). Each kidney contains about 1 million glomeruli, which pass the filtered blood through long tubules into the medulla (the central collecting region of the kidney). The glomeruli and tubules make up the nephrons, the functioning units of the kidney. As people age the number of functioning nephrons is reduced; this process may be speeded up by disease.

The main functions of the kidneys are to regulate blood and electrolytes and to eliminate waste products. The most important waste products are those generated by the breakdown of proteins. The kidneys also control the body's acid-base balance. When blood and body fluids become too acid or too alkaline, the urine acidity is altered to restore the balance. When excess water is ingested the kidney excretes it; when water is lost (as a result of diarrhea or sweating), the kidney conserves it.

The kidney also produces several hormones, including erythropoietin, which regulates the production and release of red blood cells from the bone marrow. *Vitamin D* is converted into active hormonal form by the kidney. Renin, an enzyme released by the kidney when blood pressure falls, acts on a protein in the blood to produce *angiotensin* (a powerful constrictor of small arteries that helps regulate blood pressure). Angiotensin also controls the release of aldosterone, and adrenal hormone that acts on the tubules to promote reabsorption of sodium and excretion of potassium.

KIDNEY FACTS [88]
Kidney stone formation is more prevalent in:
• Heredity - runs in families
• Men have them more frequently than women.
• More common in the tropics than Northern climes.
• Cranberry juice helps a little, but lots of water works fine.
• Don't eat too many beans, beets & berries & lay off the chocolate.

Causes - There are many causes of kidney failures, briefly they are:
1. **Drugs** - many over-the-counter painkillers, analgesics, ibuprofens and acetaminophen cause kidney problems, and stronger narcotic and steroid drugs routinely cause liver failure. In America, alcohol and prescription drugs are your twin kidney's greatest killers.
2. **Infection** - tuberculosis, generally considered a lung disease also infects your kidneys. There are many types of microorganisms that attack kidneys under the general heading of *pyelonephritis*.
3. **Genetic** - some people are just born with congential, malformed kidneys.
4. **Stones** - caused by excessive concentrations of free flowing calcium ions which crystallize into stones.

5. **Autoimmune** - lupus disease, diabetes and glameru-lenephritis all attack the kidneys.

6. **Cancer** - tumors develop to stop the flow causing tubular necrosis.

Symptoms - Problems urinating, urine discolor, pain and discomfort.

Magnetic Therapy - In France, they have had tremendous success with magnetized water which helps with kidney stones (the #1 kidney problem) in two ways. First, the water acts as a diuretic by increasing urine secretion. As an aid to good kidney health you should drink lots of water to keep the kidneys constantly flushed. Second, the power of magnetism moves calcium ions (92% of a stone) and keeps them from crystallizing into a kidney stone. Magnetized water is *not* a cure for kidney stones which are already established, but they will help stop stones from forming. [85] Dr. H.L. Bausal of Johns Hopkins Medical Center, Baltimore, Maryland, also writes of positive effects of magnetized water on the dissolving of small kidney stones. He writes that taking small quantities of magnetized water (about 50 ml) every ten minutes for eight to ten repetitions, will ease the pain of a kidney stone attack. [86]

G.S. Brila, a doctor of Ayurvedic Medicine tells of

85. Donnet, Louis, *Les Aimants pour Votre Saute (Magnets for Your Health)*, Editions dangles, St.-Jean-de-Braye, France, 1996
86. Bausal, H.L., et al., *Magneto Therapy, Self-Help Book*, J. Bain Publishers, Ltd., New Delhi, India, 1994

a patient who experienced dramatic relief from kidney pain by the application of magnetic therapy to the kidneys which induced great blood circulation; thus, lowering the pain level. [87]

In Italy, doctors found that magnetic therapy worked great on kidney infections in lowering the inflammation so the kidney returned to normal function. [89] In Russia, they found the same results on kidney infections with the therapeutic applications of magnetic therapy. [90]

As a natural health alternative, magnetic therapy can help you with the searing pain of a kidney stone attack.

87. Birla, G.S., et al., *Magnet Therapy*, Healing Arts Press, Rochester, VT, 1999
88. The Columbia University Complete Home Medical Guide, Crown Publishers, Inc., N.Y.C., NY, 1985
89. Li, A.A., et al., Magnetic Therapy with patients with Chronic Pyelonephritis, Second World Congress, Bologna, Italy, 1997
90. Rodoman, V.E., et al., *Magnetism and Experimental Inflammatory Kidney Disease*, Urology Nefol, Moscow, March 1993

LIVER DISORDER

Description - The largest and one of the most important internal organs, which functions as the body's chemical factory and regulates the levels of most of the main chemicals in blood, weighing 2.5 to 3.3 pounds the liver is a roughly cone-shaped, red-brown organ that occupies the upper right abdominal cavity. The liver lies immediately beneath the diaphragm; it has two main lobes.

The liver receives oxygenated blood from the hepatic artery and nutrient-rich blood via the portal vein (see illustration). The blood drains into the hepatic veins. The liver cells secrete *bile*, a fluid that leaves the liver through a network of ducts, the bile ducts. Within the liver, the small bile ducts and branches of the hepatic artery and the portal vein form a kind of conduit system known as the portal tracts.

Meridian/Organ	Peak period
Liver	1am-3am
Lungs	3am-5am
Large intestine	5am-7am
Stomach	7am-9am
Secretion (spleen/ pancreas)	9am-11am
Heart	11am-1pm
Small intestine	1pm-3pm
Bladder	3pm-5pm
Kidney	5pm-7pm
Heart constrictor	7pm-9pm
Vascular network	9pm-11pm
Gall bladder	11pm-1am

The liver has many functions vital to the body. One is to produce important proteins for blood plasma. They include albumin (which regulates the exchange of water between blood and tissues), complement (a group of proteins that plays a part in the *immune system's* defenses against infection), coagulation factors (which enable blood to clot when a blood vessel wall is damaged), and

97

globin (a constituent of the oxygen-carrying pigment *hemoglobin*). The liver also produces *cholesterol* and special proteins that help carry fats around the body.

Another function of the liver is to take up glucose that is not required immediately by the body's cells, and store it as glycogen. When the body needs to generate more energy and heat, the liver (under the stimulation of hormones) converts the glycogen back to glucose and releases it into the bloodstream.

The liver also regulates the blood level of amino acids, chemicals that form the building blocks of proteins. When the blood contains too high a level of amino acids (such as after a meal), the liver converts some of them

into glucose, some into proteins, some into other amino acids, and some into urea, which is passed to the kidney for excretion in the urine.

Along with the kidneys, the liver acts to clear the blood of drugs and poisonous substances that would otherwise accumulate in the bloodstream. The liver absorbs the substances to be removed from the blood, alters their chemical structure, makes them water soluble, and excretes them in the bile.

Bile carries waste products away from the liver and helps in the breakdown and absorption of fats in the small intestine.

Although extremely complex in its functions, the liver is a remarkably resilient organ. Up to three quarters of its cells can be destroyed or surgically removed before it ceases to function.

Causes - There are many causes of liver failure, briefly they are:

1. **Drugs** - America's drug of choice, alcohol causes 80% of all liver problems. Alcohol induced cirrhosis and hepatitis enlarge, inflame and destroy the majority of sick livers.

2. **Infections** - Hepatitis, cholangitis and worm/parasite disease like liver flukes, schistosomiasis and hydatid disease also claim many folks.

3. **Poisons** - Tylenol is a poison to your liver; also many mushrooms poison the liver.

4. **Metabolic** - If you have too much copper in your blood, Wilson's disease is a problem; too much iron causes hemochromatosis, and Billy the Kid caught a bullet through the liver and obviously died from lead poisoning.

> Magnetic field therapy is a method that penetrates the whole body and can treat every organ without chemical side effects.
> Wolfgang Ludwig Sc.D., Ph.D.

Symptoms - Pain in the upper right abdomen, with weight loss, loss of appetite and lethargy. In later stages you see the yellow color of jaundice discolor the whole body; especially, the eyes.

Magnetic Therapy - The liver is the largest magnetized organ in the human body and the reason is it has the greatest concentration of hemoglobin which has an iron base that is greatly affected by magnetic energy. All organs have an optimal period of activity, usually lasting for a two hour duration, ten hours of normal function and twelve hours of rest. This biorhythm is essential for the normal balance of your body and the conservation of your internal energy. The reason many drugs are bad is because they interfere with your normal 24 hour circadian rhythms which are so essential for your homeostasis (body balance). Our bodies are regulated by an internal clock which is governed by your endocrine system (the timing wheel) and the tick tock of the hormones they secrete (the second/minute/hour hands). Magnetic therapy's great contribution to your health is its ability to calm, adjust and synchronize these rhythms. The silent spark of magnetic energy keeps all your instruments (organs) functioning in beautiful unison like a well-rehearsed orchestra. [91]

The magnetic energy runs through the twelve main organ meridians of the body. Half of these organs transform outside energy into internal energy useful to the body (your digestive system which converts outside food into inside energy). The other half (heart, kidney and liver) are responsible for circulating, regulating and purifying your transportation system (your blood). [92]

By sleeping each night on a magnetic sleep system you are allowing magnetic energy to help synchronize your whole body. [93] It is the easiest way to take your medicine. You don't have to strap it on, inject it or ingest it for it to work wonders for you. All you have to do is go

91. *Thema, Encyclopedic Larousse, Sciences de la Vie (Science of Life)*, Larousse, Paris, France, 1991
92. Muller, Lise Arcand, *L'acupuncture*, Les Editions Quebecor, Outremont Quebec, Canada, 1993
93. Goldberg, Burton, *Alternative Medicine*, Future Medicine Publishing, Fife, WA, 1995

to bed each night; hopefully, something you are already doing. Using a magnetic mattress pad is the greatest way for you to benefit from this fantastic health modality. It is the natural alternative for you and your loved ones.

Lung Disorders

Description - The main organ of the *respiratory system*. The two lungs supply the body with oxygen and eliminate carbon dioxide from the blood.

The *trachea* (windpipe) branches in the chest into two main *bronchi* (air passages), which supply the left and right lungs. The main bronchi divide again into smaller bronchi and then into bronchioles, which lead to air passages that open out into grape-like air sacs called alveoli. It is through the thin walls of the alveoli that gases diffuse into or out of the blood.

Each lung is enclosed in a double membrane called the *pleura* which allows the lungs to slide freely as they expand and contract during *breathing*.

Causes - 1. Tobacco - The greatest hazard to lungs is cigarette smoking. It is the second greatest cause of cancer, which after heart attacks kills more Americans (highest among women) than any other problem. The insidious part is there is no mystery of how or why. All you need to do to make sure you don't fall victim to this hacking death is *STOP SMOKING*!

2. Infections - Pneumonia is the greatest killer here; especially among older people. Not often recognized by the medical establishment, is that much pneumonia is caught because some people breathe through their mouths and not through their noses (which is the correct way to breathe). Thus, they draw all the oral bacteria down on their fragile lungs for it to breed and cause pneumonia. There are hundreds of other types of lung infections from the common cold to killer influenza.

3. Allergies - Asthma and hayfever top the charts here but there are a lot more.

4. Injury - You can easily injure your lungs by breathing poisonous dusts, toxic gases or polluted air filled with asbestos, silica or carbon monoxide.

There are many things that can go wrong wiht your lungs and you only have about 10 minuets before you pass out and you are out of here into eternity.

Symptoms - The first signs are shortness of breath and coughing, followed by blood in your phlegm, chest pain and raspy wheezing. When you have problems with your lungs, you generally don't need a doctor or anyone else to tell you - you'll know!

Magnetic Therapy - Chronic bronchitis is a constant cough with the patient continually spitting sputum (phlegm). For some reason it effects men much more than women; although, the percentage of men smoking is dropping and women rising (America now has more female smokers - you've come a long way Baby!). Around the world it is a rising epidemic especially in Asia and Eastern Europe. Chronic bronchitis leads to *Emphysema* which together are sometimes called *Chronic Obstructive Lung Disease (COLD)* which is America's leading, killer, pulmonary disease. In Russia, they did a double-blind placebo-controlled study using magnetic therapy on COLD patients. Magnetic therapy was used in conjuncture with standard drug therapies and the group using magnets had a 20% increase in beneficial results and the positive effects showed 55% faster than in the control group not using magnet energy. [93] The reason given why magnetic therapy was so helpful was that it increased the blood flow and quickened the collection and elimination of lung toxins.

At the First International Congress on Stress, held at Montreux, Switzerland in 1988, Swedish Dr. Bjorn Nordenstrom, of Bloomington, MN, presented a paper which explained how magnetic therapy helped people with lung cancer to stop the malignant tumors from spreading (metastasizing). Dr. Nordenstrom appeared on a 20/20 television program and showed how magnetism traveled through the body's meridians and stopped the spread of this terrible cancer.[94]

In 1992, a female patient suffering terribly by chronic asthma used magnetic therapy for two months after which her asthma and breathing flow was improved by 75%. After a year of therapy she no longer needs magnetism for her asthma, but continues to use it for her insomnia.[95] Another female patient had a common cold and severely congested bronchial tubes. She used magnetic therapy and her condition improved dramatically in just two days.[96]

Magnetic therapy is a natural alternative that has helped thousands of people with problems such as the common cold, asthma, pleurisy and even lung cancer.

93. Iurlov, V.M., et al., *The Efficacy of Magnetic Therapy in Chronic Bronchitis*, Voen. Med. Zh., USSR, 1989
94. Nordenstrom, B., Congress on Stress, Montreux, Switzerland, 1988
95. Johnson, Larry, *Magnetic Healing and Meditation*, White Elephant Publishing, San Francisco, CA, 1994
96. IBID

Magnetic therapy *is not a remedy* for the original cause of these diseases which are created by germs, human biological conditions or enviromental problems (smoking, smog, etc.). What magnetic therapy does extremely well is to help your body to naturally heal itself by increase blood flow, cellular oxidation and calming/settling of the bodily systems along the meridian channels similar to the way acupuncture works. Try it - you'll like it, its easy, inexpensive and 100% safe!

MENTAL DISORDERS

Description - Our brain is our most important organ. This is true because it is the one organ that makes us who we *"are."* When John Jones gets a transplanted kidney, he is still John Jones, but if he were to get Mary Smith's brain, who is he? or her? In medicine, the brain is the least understood of all organs, and has the most problems. These mental problems are generally defined as pysciological (something goes wrong with the physical plumbing) of psychological (something goes wrong with the wiring hook-ups). Under psychological, we have two broad categories; phacolyses (complex biochemical brain disease) and neuroses (related to upbringing and personality. Some problems that are in our head are Alzheimer's, Epilepsy, Headaches, Insomnia and Parkinson's which are discussed in other sections of this book. In this heading, we will learn about how magnetic therapy helps with Depression, Schizophrenia, Attention Deficit Disorder (ADD), Jet Lag, Anxiety and Stress.

Causes - The causes of mental disorders are myriad. They encompass all potential stimulations from nutrition to pollution, from heredity to identity, from infections to injuries and from pharmaceutical medications to unknown. To make the causal equation often more difficult, many disorders have more than one cause in a complicated mental matrix.

Symptoms - Just as the causes are so varied, so too are the symptoms. Mental disorders exhibit such a range of complex emotions from vague feelings of personality differences to the empty hollowness of coma - like vegetation of mind and spirit. There are, unfortunately, no set of standard symptoms like diabetics or arthritis which can be easily diagnosed.

Magnetic Therapy - Attention Deficit Disorder (ADD) has often been called *"the disease of the year"* because of its recent, dramatic rise in inflicting our children, predominantly boys. It is characterized by hyperactivity, restlessness, unfocused behavior and impulsiveness. Thousands of these children are given Ritalin, a very strong, psycho-stimulant which when taken by non-ADD people *causes* hypertension, but with ADD people it paradoxically has a calming effect. The reason we believe for this unusual phenomena is that ADD's

neurotransmitters move to different brain receptors. ADD children often appear to exhibit low self-esteem and seem confused. Many of them are brilliant because their minds seem to work faster, and they develop different problem solving approaches not quickly understood by the vast majority of non-ADD people. If an ADD can overcome their inability to concentrate and focus, they can become extremely effective. Both Edison and Einstein were ADD, both had terrible times as adolescents in school and were considered retarded, and both changed our modern technology more than any other two people.

A tremendous breakthrough in ADD research was conducted by Dr. Bernard Margolis of Harrisburg, Pennsylvania. When Dr. Margolis administered Ritalin to teenage ADD patients he was very upset with the horrendous side effects of depressed appetite slower physical growth, sleep problems and an emotional roller coaster between aggressive and depressive behavior caused by the drug. Although he originally thought magnetic therapy was a bunch of old wives tales with no scientific basis, he was amazed when a grandmother speeded the recovery of burns to her four-year-olds hands by use of magnets.

Dr. Margolis decided to use magnetic therapy on 30 children (2 girls, 28 boys) aged 5 to 18 with ADD. He took them all off Ritalin, and after receiving parental consent, put all on magnetic therapy with mattress pads at night and shoe insoles during the day, and all continued their strict nutritional diet to help ADD's sufferers. Of the 30, two dropped out, 9 had no marginal differences than when they were using Ritalin but by 19 had dramatic results which justified and legitimized the beneficial results of the magnetic therapy. [97]

In another study conducted by Dr. Lawrence and Dr. Rosch, is on the relationship of depression and stress

97. Lawrence, R., et al., *Magnet Therapy, the Pain Cure Alternative*, Prima Health Publishing, rocklin, CA, 1998

which the National Institute of Mental Health calls a *"chicken and egg enigma"* because it's difficult to diagnose which comes first. Over $50 billion was spent in America in 2000 on depression, so it is a tremendous problem effecting women on a 60% vs 40% greater scale. The side effects of drugs like Prozac include nervousness, anxiety, agitation, insomnia, nightmares, anorexia, impotence, and an overall manic state of mind. A new magnetic therapy called repetitive Transcranial Magnetic Stimulation (rTMS) has been used very successfully. Dr. Mark George of Washington's *National Institute of Health* found that rTMS helped relieve depression without drugs.[98]

New Brain Anyone?
A joint project of IBM and Motorola has developed a cranial computer. They have already built a working model that spans the space between the skull and the cerebrum. The problem is not with its construction, but with its connections to the brain's soft tissue. Many new strategic breakthroughs have been made in the interface connections, and it looks feasible for the first human to have a computer-aided brain within the decade. A cinch for "Who Wants to be a Millionaire."

This Trancranial Magnetic Stimulation (TMS) device was first developed by the research team of John Rothwell and Pat Merton at London's *Institute of Neurology* in the early 1990's. It works by stimulating the magnetic energy which revives the neural activity of the brain which has been numbed by people suffering from chronic depression. Besides helping people snap out of depression, it is also used to diagnose Parkinson's, strokes and brain tumors. [99.]

TMS applications for neuropsychiatry are gaining wide acceptance in Australia, Israel, Switzerland,

98. George, Mark, *Happiness is a Magnet*, New Scientist, August, 1995
99. Coghill, Roger, *The book of Magnetic Healing*, Simon & Schuster, London, UK, 2000

Germany and the United Kingdom. American doctors however, have shown little motivation to stop prescribing powerful pharmaceuticals for depression stress and anxiety. One exception is Dr. Pascual-Leone of Harvard Medical School and a researcher at Beth Israel Deaconess Hospital. He treated severely depressed patients who showed no response to drugs. After a 10 day course of treatments, 50% felt therapeutic benefits where they had none with drugs. [100]

In an Israeli research, reported to the Archives of General Psychiatry, a group of 70 severely depressed patients were divided. Of the rTMS patients 49% experienced major improvement while only 25% showed improvement on a drug therapy. [101]

Schizophrenia is another major mental disorder helped by magnetic therapy. Dr. Ralph Hoffman of Yale University Medical School worked with twelve auditory hallucinations (Schizophrenics often hear "voices" telling them what to do) patients. One got no stoppage of the voices, three received them less frequently, and eight got total stoppage. However, without

Mental Confusion Linked to Swollen Bladder

Older folks may become confused for many reasons. But new research suggests an unexpected link between confusion and urine retention in studies of 3 men over the age of 70.

Because of urinary problems, these men retained too much urine in their bladders. As a result, the men rapidly became confused, shaky and unable to communicate.

When doctors treated the 3 to relieve urine retention, the men's confusion disappeared. Urine retention is a possible cause for unexplained mental confusion.

Archives of Internal Medicine (150,12:2577)

100. Pascual, Lone A., et al., *TMS for Depression for Drug-Resistant Patients,* Lancet, UK, 1996
101. *TMS for Depression,* The Integretive Medical Consultant, 1:10, 1999

the continued use of magnetic therapy all had return of the voices within 4 days to two months. [102]

Dr. Larry Johnson gives many examples of his patients receiving excellent results from depression through the use of magnetic therapy in his book, *Magnetic Healing and Meditation*, some of which appear in the individual testimonies of his book. [103]

Another mental disorder which causes minor depression, confusion, lethargy and general disorientation, which is helped dramatically by magnetic therapy, is jet lag. It sounds almost comical, but when you travel rapidly around the planet your relationship with Earth's geomagnetic field becomes disorientated. When you stay put for three days your natural relationship with the Earth's field will return to normal, but if you are *constantly* on the go, some people have difficulty continually resetting their biorhythms and internal circadian clock. Magnetic therapy acts like a videotape eraser,

Phosphate deficiency linked to Hallucinations

One 59-year-old woman suffered from frightening visual hallucinations for two days. This lady was admitted to the hospital for diabetes and, she was alert and mentally aware.

However, after 24 hours, she began suffering from frightening hallucination. She had no history of mental problems or of alcohol or drug abuse. The medical staff tested her blood and found she was suffering from a deficiency of phosphorus.

They immediately started her on phosphorus replacement treatment, and the hallucinations disappeared within 4 hours.

She had been suffering from a phosphorus deficiency known as "hypophosphatemia." If you experience visual or auditory (hearing) hallucinations, see your doctor immediately and ask him to test your blood phosphorus level.

102. Hoffman, R.E., *TMS and Auditory Hallucinations in Schizophrenia*, Lancet, UK, 2000
103. Johnson, Larry, Magnetic Healing and Meditation, White Elephant Publishing, San Francisco, CA, 1988

and allows both your daily circadian and your monthly Biorhythms to adjust much more rapidly when you are traveling. One British stewardess who flew regularly from England to Australia was about to quit because of menstrual deviations, but returned to normal with magnetic therapy and happily kept her job. [104]

In Russia, where the winter nights seem to last forever, environmental depression is a common problem, almost epidemic. Research has shown that magnetic therapy stimulates the pineal gland which in turn secretes more melatonin. This melatonin, besides from its proven abilities as an antioxidant (the brain's only natural antioxidant), calming effector and sleep inducer, also acts as a natural antidepressant. People who suffer from Seasonal Affective Disorder (SAD - lack of sunlight) are dramatically helped by magnetic therapy. [105]

When It's Time to Seek Help

If you're feeling down and out and the feeling persists - even though you've tried all you know to beat it - it may be time to see a mental health professional. Experts at the National Institute for Mental Health suggest that anyone who experiences four or more of the following symptoms for more than two weeks should seek help.

• Persistent sad, anxious, or "empty" feelings.
• Feelings of hopelessness and/or pessimism.
• Feelings of guilt, worthlessness, and/or helplessness.
• Loss of interest or pleasure in ordinary activities, including sex.
• Sleep disturbances (including insomnia, early-morning waking, and/or oversleeping).
• Eating disturbances (changes in appetite and/or weight loss or gain).
• Decreased energy, fatigue and/or a feeling of being "slowed down."
• Thoughts of death or suicide, or suicide attempts.
• Restlessness and/or irritability.
• Difficulty in concentrating, remembering and/or making decisions.

Doctor's Book of Home Remedies

104. Coghill, Roger, *The Book of Magnet Healing*, Simon and Schuster, London, UK, 2000

TMS experiments were also tried in Italy with great therapeutic results. A large study of depressed patients showed that 51% had significant improvement, 41% showed some improvement and 8%had no improvement.[106]

Anxiety and stress are twin killers in today's rat race would. Most people prefer to avoid much of the tranquilizing drugs that proliferate the pharmacies of our land because they don't want to get hooked on the addictiveness nor do they want to give up their lives to a drug-induced LA-LA Land of chemical dependency. The problem remains because anxiety and stress stimulate the adrenal glands to secrete excessive amounts of cortisol. Like its chemical cousin adrenaline (both born in the same adrenal glands) cortisol makes you jumpy

BIORHYTHMS
Human hormones of Endocrine system have a monthly ebb and flo matching the moon's cycles. The three types are Intellectual (33 days), Emotional (28 days) and Physical (23 days). Certain days are more critical than others. Menstruation is but one example.

and prepares you for "flight or fight syndrome." But, cortisol is stronger and literally attacks your body from within by destroying your immune system (Cushing's syndrome), killing brain cells, weakening your heart through atherosclerosis, and greatly accelerating your aging process. Cortisol is nothing to mess with for it will lead you to an early grave.[107]

105. Sandyk, R., et al; Magnetic Therapy, International Journal for Neuoscience, June 1991
106.Comea, A., et al; TMS, a Novel Antidepressive Strategy, Neuropsychobiology, 1996
107. Segala, Melanie, *Disease Prevention and Treatment, Edition III,* Life Extension Media, Ft. Lauderdale, FL. 2000

How does magnetic therapy help relieve anxiety and stress? There is no pain outside the brain. This means that only your brain has the capacity to understand and interpret pain signals sent to it by the injured part of your body. If you cut your finger, a pain signal is sent to the brain. If that signal is interrupted or not processed by the brain, you will never know that your finger is cut. Magnetic energy through the acupuncture point P6 (Chinese Nei-Kuan) registers stress in your brain (thalamus, part of limbic system in the core of your brain). The limbic system is the part of your brain that receives emotional responses and in turn acts upon them. Magnetic Therapy either lessens or totally interferes with the stress impulses as they are sent; thus, you remain calm and don't overreact to the anxiety. [108]

Circadian Rhythm
This is your internal clock set by the Sun's dawn and dusk. This 24 hr. cycle controls sleeping & waking, mood & behavior, eating, body temperature and concentration. Keeping a steady, daily pace, keeps you regular and effective. Shift workers have problems.

Most Americans head for the medicine cabinet when they feel anxious or stressed, this is a bad route to travel for these medicines only mask the symptoms never dealing with the causes. These artificial, synthetic drugs also come with side effects that last longer than any beneficial help they provided. Magnetic Therapy also does not solve the causes of your anxiety and stress - only you can solve your problems. However, magnetism is the natural health alternative that 100% safely relieves your problem without all the damaging drug side effects.

---

108. Lawrence, Ron, et al; *Magnet Therapy, The Pain Cure Alternative*, Prima health, Rocklin, CA, 1998

MULTIPLE SCLEROSIS

Description - A progressive disease of the central nervous system in which scattered patches of myelin (the protective covering of nerve fibers) in the brain and spinal cord are destroyed. This causes symptoms ranging from numbness and tingling to paralysis and incontinence. The severity of multiple sclerosis (MS) varies markedly among sufferers.

Causes - The cause of multiple sclerosis remains unknown. It is thought to be an autoimmune disease in which the body's defense system begins to treat the myelin in the central nervous system as foreign, gradually destroying it, with subsequent scarring and damage to some of the underlying nerve fibers.

When Stress Threatens
Too much stress can directly threaten your health. Paul J. Rosch, M.D., says that any of the following stress-related symptoms may indicate that you should seek medical help promptly.
- Dizzy spells or blackouts
- Rectal bleeding (may indicate an ulcer)
- A racing pulse that won't stop
- Sweaty palms
- Chronic back and neck pain
- Chronic or severe headaches
- Trembling
- Hives
- Overwhelming anxiety
- Insomnia
"The basic rule is this: You should see a doctor if the symptoms you're experiencing are new and have no obvious cause, especially if they interfere with your quality of life." Dr. Rosch says.
Doctor's Book of Home Remedies

There seems to be a genetic factor since relatives of affected people are eight times more likely than others to contact the disease. Environment may also play a part - it is five times more common in temperate zones (such as the US and Europe) than in the tropics. Spending the first 15 years of life in a particular area seems to

115

determine future risk. It is thought that a virus picked up by a susceptible person during this early period of life may be responsible for the disease's later development.

Multiple sclerosis is the most common acquired (not present at birth) disease of the nervous system in young adults. In relatively high-risk temperate areas the incidence is about one in every 1,000 people. The ratio of women to men sufferers is 2 to 1.

Symptoms - Multiple sclerosis usually starts in early adult life. It may be active briefly and then resume years later. The symptoms vary with which parts of the brain and spinal cord are affected.

Spinal cord damage can cause tingling, numbness, or a feeling of constriction in any part of the body. The extremities may feel heavy and become weak. *Spasticity* (stiffness) sometimes develops. The nerve fibers to the bladder may be involved, causing incontinence.

Damage to the white matter in the brain may lead to fatigue, vertigo, clumsiness, muscle weakness, slurred speech, unsteady gait, blurred or double vision, and numbness, weakness, or pain in the face.

These symptoms may occur singly or in combination and may last from several weeks to several months. In some sufferers, relapses may be precipitated by injury infection, or physical or emotional stress.

Attacks vary considerably in their severity from person to person. In some, the disease may consist of mild relapses and long symptom-free periods throughout life, with very few permanent effects. Others have a series of flare-ups, leaving them with some disability, but further deterioration ceases. Some become gradually more disabled from the first attack and are bedridden and incontinent in early middle life. A small group suffers gross disability within the first year.

A person disabled with multiple sclerosis may have problems in addition to the paralysis, such as painful muscle spasms, urinary tract infections, constipation, skin ulceration, and changes of mood between euphoria and depression.

MS UNUSUAL FACTS
There is no known cause for MS. Heredity, environment and possible viruses are suspect, but not proven. It effects Northern European Caucasians mostly. If you were to draw a line along the 37° latitude (NC/Virginia border to mid-California) the chance of getting MS are twice that north of this border than south, for the exact same population genetics. We don't have a clue why!

There is no single diagnostic test for multiple sclerosis; confirmation of the disease is usually the exclusion of all other possible conditions. A neurologist may perform tests to help confirm the diagnosis, including *lumbar puncture* (removal of a sample of fluid from the spinal cord for laboratory analysis), or using MRI, the use of which, magnetic field verifies MS.

Magnetic Therapy - In Russia, many studies have been performed on MS patients using magnetic therapy because MS is common there and magnetic therapy is inexpensive to use. [109, 110, 111]

109. Sandyk, R. & Derpapas, K., *Successful Treatment of MS by Magentic Therapy*, International Journal of Neuroscience, May 1993.
110. Sandyk, R., *Magnetic Fields Improve Body Functions of MS Pa tients*, Internationa Journal of Neuroscience, June 1995
111. Sandyk, R. & Iacono, R.P., *MS Improvement with Magnetic Therapy*, International Journal of Neuroscience, Feb. 1996

In Hungary, the symptoms of an MS patient were alleviated by the use of magnetic therapy. [112]

In France, more double-blind, placebo-controlled studies were done on MS individuals suffering from cerebral paralysis. The magnetic therapy helped them regain some body control and locomotion. [113]

Dr. Todd Richards and Dr. Martha Lappin of the University of Washington did a double-blind study on 30 multiple sclerosis patients. The half that got the real magnetic therapy showed dramatic improvement in bladder control, cognitive function, fatigue levels, mobility and vision. [114]

Roger MacDougall
In 1953, this famous play-wright, composer and musician was diagnosed with MS. His condition worsened until he was a complete invalid in a wheelchair. He tried a hun-ger/gather diet, no white flour, no fat, no sugar and no processed food at all - everything fresh. He only used natural supplements and exercised as best he could. By 1975, he was completely cured of MS, and died healthy in his late 80's.
Life Extension

In Latvia, Dr. R. Kikut treated 1,000 patients with multiple sclerosis which caused aneurysms and he found life-saving beneficial results from magnetic therapy. This natural alternative can help with one of the most devastating diseases, MS, known to medicine.

---

112. Guseo, A., *Magnetic Therapy used on MS in Double-Blind Cross-over Study*, Journal of Biolelectricity, 1987
113. Sieron, a., et al; *Magnetic Therapy Works in Complex Neurological Diseases*, European BioElectromagnetics Assn., Nancy, France, 1996
114. Richards, T.L., Lappin, M.S., etal; *Double Blind Study using Magnetic Therapy on MS*, Journal Alternative Complementary Medicine, 1996

NEUROPATHY

Description - Disease, inflammation, or damage to the peripheral nerves, which connect the central nervous system, or CNS (brain and spinal cord), to the sense organs, muscles, glands, and internal organs. Symptoms caused by neuropathies include numbness, tingling, pain, or muscle weakness, depending on the nerves affected.

Most nerve cell axons (the conducting fibers that make up nerves) are insulated within a sheath of a fatty substances called myelin, but some are unmyelinated. Most neuropathies arise from damage or irritation either to the axons or to their myelin sheaths. An axon may suffer thinning, complete loss of, or patchy loss of its myelin sheath. This may cause a slowing or a complete block to the passage of electrical signals.

FAT and MS
There has been a strong correlation between fat intake and MS. People who eat red meat, butter, milk and cheese have MS much more often. A Norwegian study showed that inferior people whose diet was fat reindeer meat had 8 times MS than coastal Norwegians who ate mostly fish protein. Also, Southern Italians whose fat comes mostly from olive oil never get MS.
Life Extension

Some neuropathies are described according to their underlying cause (e.g., diabetic neuropathy and alcoholic neuropathy).

Neuralgia described pain cause by irritation or inflammation of a particular nerve.

Causes - In some cases of neuropathy there is no obvious or detectable cause. Among the many specific causes are *diabetes mellitus*, dietary deficiencies (particularly of B vitamins), persistent excessive alcohol consumption, and metabolic upsets such as *uremia*. Other causes include *leprosy, lead poisoning*, or poisoning by drugs.

Nerves may become acutely inflamed. This often occurs after a viral infection (for example, in *Guillain-Barre syndrome*). Neuropathies may result from autoimmune disorders such as *rheumatoid arthritis*, systemic *lupus erythematosus, or periarteritis nodosa.* In these disorders, there is often damage to the blood vessels supplying the nerves. Neuropathies may occur secondarily to malignant tumors such as *lung cancer*, or with *lymphomas* and *leukemias.* Finally, there is a group of inherited neuropathies, the most common being *peroneal muscular atrophy.*

Symptoms - The symptoms of neuropathy depend on whether it affects mainly sensory nerve fibers or motor nerve fibers. Damage to sensory nerve fibers may cause numbness and tingling, sensations of cold, or pain, often starting in the hands and feet and spreading toward the body center. Damage to motor fibers may cause muscle weakness and muscle wasting.

Damage to nerves of the autonomic nervous system may lead to blurred vision, impaired or absent seating, episodes of faintness associated with falls in blood

CUBAN EPIDEMIC
From 1991 to 1993, Cuba had neuropathies affecting nearly 51,000 people. The main neuropathies were causing problems with vision, hearing and memory loss. Upon investigation, the reason for the wide spread nerve problems were lack of proper food; speci?cally, lack of Vitamin B_{12} and folic Acid (another type of Vit. B). The problem was accelerated by heavy smoking (cigars in particular) and alcohol consumption. The epidemic eased with massive Vitamin B supplements.
New England Jour. of Med Nov. 2, 1995

pressure, and disturbance of gastric, intestinal, bladder, and sexual functioning, including incontinence and impotence. Some neuropathies are linked with particular symptoms (for example, very painful neuropathies may arise in diabetes mellitus and in alcohol dependence).

Magnetic Therapy - Dr. Margaret Patterson's electromagnetic therapy set up magnetic fields in the brain which lowered neuropathies brought about by drug abuse of heroin, cocaine, morphine and amphetamines. [115]

In Hungary, 148 neurologically impaired patients in an Hungarian hospital were studied for 3 years. In the study, the patients had a 58% to 80% improvement in their conditions of neurological or locomotor disorders. [116]

In Russia, a study confirmed beneficial results on polyneuropathies in 25 out of 27 patients receiving treatment. [117]

Diseases to your nervous system range from inconvenient tics, to painful inflammations to ultimate death. These illnesses are difficult to diagnose because there are so many possible culprits in our modern society with processed foods, legal and illegal drugs and polluted environment. However, there are natural alternatives available to you to save your nerves and your life.

115. Lawrence, Ron; et al, *Magnet Therapy, The Pain Cure Alternative*, Prima Publishing, Rocklin, CA, 1998
116. Terlaki, G.; *Clinical Experiences by Magnetic Therapy*, Hungarian Symposium on Magnetotherapy, Budapest, Hungary, May 1987.
117. Shiman, A.G.; et al; *Combined Treatments Using Magnetotherapy on Polinveropathies*, Vopr Kurortol izioter Lech Fiz Kult, 1993

PAIN

Description - A localized sensation that can range from mild discomfort to an unbearable and excruciating experience. Pain is the result of stimulation of special sensory nerve endings following injury or caused by disease.

The skin contains many specialized nerve endings (nociceptors). Stimulation of these receptors leads to the transmission of pain messages to the brain. Nociceptors have different sensitivities, some responding only to severe stimulation, such as cutting, pricking, or heating the skin to a high temperature; others respond to warning stimuli, such as firm pressure, stretching, or temperatures not high enough to burn. Pain receptors are present in structures other than the skin including blood vessels and tendons. Most internal organs have few, if any, nociceptors. The large intestine, for example, can be cut without causing any pain. It does, however, have nociceptors that respond to stretching, which, in severe cases, may cause pain.

FLORIDA Neuropathies
Florida hospitals noted an increase in patients coming down with painful neuropathies who also were on cholesterol-lowering drugs. These "statin" prescribed pharmaceuticals included:
Lovastatin
Siarvastatin
Pravastatin
Atorvastatin
An FDA warning went out for doctors to lower their Rx scripts for these drugs.
South. Med. Journal
July 1998

Causes - Pain is usually associated with distress and anxiety and sometimes with fear. People vary tremendously in their pain thresholds (the level at which the pain is felt and the person feels compelled to act). The cause and circumstances of the pain may also affect the way it is perceived by the sufferer. The pain of cancer, because of fear of the disease, may seem much greater and cause more suffering than similar pain resulting from persistent indigestion. Unexplained pain is often worse because of the anxiety it can cause; once a diagnosis is made and reassurance given, the pain may be perceived as less severe.

The experience of pain may be reduced by arousal (e.g., an injury sustained during competitive sport or on the battlefield may go unnoticed in the heat of the moment); strong emotion can also block pain.

When Pain is a Sign of Disease
A sudden muscle cramp, strain, or even extreme soreness can launch you into the pain galaxy. Sometimes it hurts so badly, you think you'll never come back to earth. Most of the time the pain is a lot more serious than the injury. But not always. Cramping, for example, could be the result of a nerve injury, says Allan Levy, M.D. Or in rare cases, it could be the result of Phlebitis - inflammation of a vein. A strain may not even be what it seems. "This is very rare," Dr. Levy says, "but I had a patient who thought he had badly strained a thigh muscle on a stationary bike. It didn't ever get better and we finally did surgery. He has a huge malignant tumor in the muscle." The point here isn't to scare you but to remind you that muscle problems that take on abnormal characteristics and linger may be more serious. Consult your doctor.

Some people believe that mental preparation for pain (e.g., in childbirth or in experiments to test pain) can greatly reduce the response.

A person's response to pain is greatly modified by past experience; the outcome of previous episodes of pain may affect the way the individual copes with subsequent pain. Factors such as insomnia, anxiety and depression, which often accompany incapacitating illness, lower pain tolerance. Treatment for these symptoms is given along with treatment for the pain to allow the minimum dose for pain relief.

Cultural differences exist in the expression of pain. In some parts of the world self-inflicted torture and the ability to withstand great pain are a mark of a person's strength and character. However, the pain of even mild torture inflicted by captors may be perceived as much worse than a similar degree of pain that occurs under different circumstances.

Symptoms - Many adjectives are used to describe different types of pain. Common descriptive terms include throbbing, penetrating, gnawing, aching, burning and gripping. The extent to which a patient is accurately able to describe his or her pain to the physician is highly variable, even though it can be a vital clue to the diagnosis.

WESTERN INTRODUCTION

Chinese immigrants brought acupuncture to America in the mid-1800's, but it was largely ignored until 1972 when James Reston, a respected New York Times columnist, underwent an emergency appendectomy while in Chine. Reston reported on the amazing postsurgical pain relief he enjoyed via a few well-placed acupuncture needles. This report attracted the attention of the American medical community, and many physicians traveled to China to observe for themselves the use of acupuncture for pain relief. They discovered that acupuncture is part of a complex, integrated healing system that goes far beyond pain relief can treat a variety of conditions, including diseases of the eyes, nerves, muscles, heart and the organs of digestion and reproduction. By the end of the 1970's, acupuncture schools and practitioners could be found throughout America, supported by dozens of professional associations and publications.

Attempts have been made to categorize pain according to intensity, ranging from a minor cut or sore throat at the lower end to childbirth and renal or biliary colic at the upper.

ACUPUNCTURE

In 1979, David Eisenberg, M.D., was invited to the Beijing Neurosurgical Institute in China to witness and assist in a major surgical operation carried out using only acupuncture for the relief of pain. The patient was a 58-year-old university professor with a brain tumor located near his pituitary gland. The neurosurgeon, Dr. Wang Zhong-cheng, recommended acupuncture analgesia because it had significantly fewer side effects than other anesthetic treatments. Throughout a 4 hour operation that included the removal of a portion of the skull to reach the tumor, the patient remained fully conscious, alert and relaxed. He received only a mild preoperative sedative, and the acupuncture consisted of the insertion of 5 needles attached to a low-voltage battery. He felt no pain and his pulse and blood pressure remained stable. When the surgery was completed, the patient stood up, thanked the surgeon, and walked out of the operating room without help.

If the pain comes from an internal organ it is often difficult for the sufferer to pinpoint its origin with any precision. For example, in the early stages of appendicitis, pain may be felt in the region about the navel. In the later stages, when infection has caused inflammation of the peritoneum (lining of the abominal cavity), the pain becomes localized about the right groin.

Pain may be felt at a point some distance from the disorder. This is called *referred pain*. A person who has lost a limb may experience pain that seems to come from the amputated limb (see *Phantom limb*). Sometimes the person can localize the pain (e.g., to a toe, despite having had a mid-thigh amputation). See also *Endorphins; Enkephalins*.

Magnetic Therapy - Pain and its management have been with us since the first mother gave birth. The first book on the subject *Nei Ching* (The Yellow Emperor's Classic of Internal Medicine) was written in China in

200 BC. The Chinese knew that pain traveled along 12 major body meridians (energy pathways) and each linked internal organ systems, along this meridian system there are over one thousand acupoints which can be stimulated to enhance the flow of *qi* (or Japanese *chi*) which is your life force enabling you to function.

These meridians are independent of your cardio-vascular, lymphatic and nervous systems; although, they are all interrelated and must coordinate for an overall healthy body. These meridians can be stimulated by needles (acupuncture), pressure (acupressure), burning (moxibustion), electricity (electro-acupuncture) and magnets (magnetic therapy). The Chinese were the first to use magnetic therapy in conjunction with the life force of the meridians over 4,000 years ago.

Magnetic acupuncture has proven to be a very successful treatment for pain relief, as it appears to stimulate the release of endorphins and enkephalins, the body's natural pain-killing chemicals. [118] David Eisenberg, M.D., Clinical Research Fellow at Harvard Medical School states that, "There is evidence that acupuncture influences the production and distribution of a great many neurotransmitters (substances that transmit nerve impulses to the brain) and neuromodulators (substance produced by neurons which affect neurotransmitters), and that this in turn alters the perception of pain." [119] In 1983 the medical journal *Pain* reviewed a number of studies that

118. Chatfield, K.B. *"The Scientific Basis of Acupuncture."* In the Textbook of Natural Medicine, ed. J.D. Pizzorno and m.T. Murray, Seattle, WA, John Bastyr College Publications, 1988.
119. Eisenberg, D., M.D., and Wright, T.L. , *Encounters with Qi: Exploring Chinese Medicine*, 2d ed. New York; Penguin Books, 1987,77.

provide further evidence of acupuncture's importance as an alternative to conventional analgesic (pain-relieving) medication. [120] In one study of over 20,000 patients at the University of California at Los Angeles, acupuncture reduced both the frequency and severity of muscle tension headaches and migraines. [121] Another study involving 204 patients suffering from chronic painful conditions, resulted in 74 percent experiencing significant pain relief for over three months after acupuncture treatments. [122] Other studies show that younger patients are particularly helped by acupuncture for the treatment of various types of pain. [123]

Endorphin Discovery
In the early 1970's, researchers at Johns Hopkins studying morphine drug use found that the human brain had morphine receptors but morphine comes from poppies, which are plants; so how did our brains develop these receptors? It was soon discovered that our bodies produce endorphins which chemically match morphine. This endorphin production in our body is naturally stimulated by magnetic energy, this is how magnets relieve pain.
Univ. of Chicago
School of Medicine
1978 Study

In America, there have been three famous studies on magnetic therapy's ability to relieve pain. They are Dr. Michael I. Weintraub's New York Medical School's study with diabetics and their peripheral neuropathy pain in their feet and legs. Dr. Agatha Colbert's study with fibromyalgia pain at Tufts University School of Medicine in Boston, and Dr. Carlton Hazelwood and Dr. Carlos Vallbona study at Baylor College of Medicine

120. Lewith, G.T., and Machine, D. *"On the Evaluation of the Clinical Effects of Acupuncture."* Pain 16 (Jun. 1983); 111-127.
121. Millman, B., *"Acupuncture: Context and Critique."* Annual Review of Medicine 28 (1977); 223-236.
122. Cheung, J. *"Effect of Electroacupuncture on Chronic Painful Conditions in General Medical Practice - A Four-Year's Study."* American Journal of Chinese Medicine 13 (1985); 33-38.
123. Sodipo, J. *"Therapeutic Acupuncture for Chronic Pain."* Pain 7 (1979); 359-365.

on severe knee pain.

Peripheral nerves are the long nerves that extend out from the spinal column and connect your limbs to the central nervous system. These fragile nerves can easily

Let's surprise everybody with a great drug that has _good_ side effects. It will drive the FDA crazy!

be damaged by toxic substances (drugs, poisons), alcoholism, AIDS, but the most common cause is diabetes. When neuropathy to these nerves occurs the person has loss of balance, muscle weakness, extreme sensitivity to touch, and lots and lots of pain. Most diabetics take antidepressants, narcotic analgesics and anticonvulsants; and most do not work real well, but leave the diabetic with more troublesome side effects to further deal with on top of the constant throbbing pain, usually in the legs. The Weintraub study had 24 initial patients, of which 19 completed the 4 month trial. Of the diabetic patients 90% had dramatic beneficial results. [124]

Fibromyalgia is an illness characterized by severe muscle pain. Many doctors misdiagnose this as chronic fatigue syndrome (CFS) or arthritis, but it is different. Fibromyalgia has deep muscle and skeletal pain where CFS does not. Arthritis has inflammation and swelling of the joints, fibromyalgia doesn't have these symptoms. Although, there is no known cause for fibromyalgia, there are many suspects. Top candidates are infections, genetics, autoimmune diseases and exposure to drugs, particularly daily usage of marijuana. Women are affected more then men by approximately 65% vs 35%. Dr. Colbert's study at Tufts was with 35 initial patients, all women suffering from fibromyalgia pain, 25 finished. All suffered for at least 2 years. The mean age was 49.7 years (youngest 25, oldest 78) average weight was 166 lbs. (115 lbs. to 216 lbs.) and all met the criteria for fibromyalgia designated by the American college of Rheumatology.[125] The subjects were divided, half slept on magnetized mattress pads, the others slept on pads with ceramic dominos, not magnets. Neither the subjects or the researchers knew which was which. After 4 months, the results were dramatic. The 13 on magnets had significant benefits, the other 12 none.[126]

Knee pain can be severe, ask any hockey, soccer or

124. Weintraub, M.I.; *Magnetic Bio-stimulation in Painful Diabetic Peripheral Neuropathy*, Am. Journal of Pain Management, 1991
125. Wolfe, F., et al, *Fibromyalgia Classification Guidelines,* Arthritis Rheumatoloy, 1990
126. Colbert, A.P., et al., *Magnetic Mattress Pad Use in Fibromyalgia Patients*, Journal of Back and Musculosketetal Rehabilitation, 1999

football player who hurt his/her knee. In the famous Hansen study done in Scandinavia in 1938, of 26 patients, we had huge benefits from magnetic therapy. [127] From this study, came the Baylor University study.

Polio is a terrible viral disease which fortunately for us has been defeated by the Salk/Sabine vaccine. However, there are thousands alive today who have had this dreadful disease, and they live in constant, chronic muscular pain. Dr. Carlton Hazelwood, a brilliant organism physiologist and one of the original designers of the Magnetic Resonance Imaging (MRI) machine pursued with Dr. Carlos Vallbona, both with the Baylor College of Medicine of Houston, Texas, this study of 50 patients with post-polio syndrome. In Arthritis Today, Vallbona stated "There's no question in my mind that magnets hold great promise." The Baylor Study proved conclusively that magnetic therapy works to reduce pain. [128]

There are a great deal more studies done on the alleviation of pain by the use of magnetic therapy; especially, outside the USA where magnets are much more commonly used. Pain relief is just one more way that natural alternatives by using magnetic therapy is making this a better world.

127. Hansen, K.M., *Influence of Magnetism on the Human Organism*, Academy of Medicine, Scandinavia, 1938
128. Vallbona, C.; Hazelwood,l d.F., Juida, G., *Response of Pain to Static Magnetic Fields in Post-Polio Patients*; a Double-Blind Pilot Study, Arch. Phys. Med. Rehabil., 1997

PARKINSON'S DISEASE

Description - A brain disorder that causes muscle tremor, stiffness and weakness. The characteristic signs are trembling, a rigid posture, slow movements, and a shuffling, unbalanced walk.

Causes - Parkinson's disease is caused by degeneration of or damage to nerve cells within the basal ganglia in the brain. The way this affects muscle tension and movement is shown in the illustrated box at left.

About one person in 200 (mostly elderly) is affected by the disease, with 50,000 new cases a year in the US. Men are more likely to be affected than women. The incidence of Parkinson's disease is lower among smokers.

Symptoms - The disease usually begins as a slight tremor of one hand, arm, or leg. In the early stages, the tremor is worse when the hand or limb is at rest.; when it is used, the shaking virtually stops.

Later, the disease affects both sides of the body and causes stiffness and weakness, as well as trembling, of the muscles. Symptoms include a stiff, shuffling, over-balancing walk that may break into uncontrollable, tiny, running steps; a constant trembling of the hands, more marked at rest and sometimes accompanied by shaking of the head; a permanent rigid stoop; and an unblinking, fixed expression. Eating, washing, dressing, and other everyday activities gradually become very difficult to manage.

The intellect is unaffected until late in the disease, although speech may become slow and hesitant; handwriting usually becomes very small. Depression is common.

Although there is no cure for Parkinson's disease, much can be done for sufferers to improve their morale and mobility through exercise, special aids in the home, and encouragement. Organizations exist to provide help and advice for suffers and their families. This is often all that is needed in the early stages of the disease.

Untreated, the disease progresses over 10 to 15 years to severe weakness and incapacity. However, with modern drug treatment, a person suffering from Parkinson's disease can obtain considerable relief from the illness and a much improved quality of life. About one third of patients do eventually show signs of *dementia.*

Experimentation with transplantation of dopamine-secreting adrenal tissue is now taking place.

Magnetic Therapy - When severely inflicted (end stage) a Parkinson's patient has an MRI done with 20,000 gauss of magnetic energy, they are temporarily cured of the tremors and appear normal for 24-48 hours until the shaking comes back. If they could receive this treatment at this strength continuously, their condition would disappear. Unfortunately, our magnetic technology has not gotten that far as yet, but at least we know the direction.

However, standard magnetic therapy is a relief for

Parkinson's victims whose conditions are not yet terminal. A 73-year-old male Parkinson's patient suffering from disabling resting and postural tremors in the right hand plus other traditional symptoms was greatly helped by a series of magnetic therapy treatments. [129]

TMS has also been very helpful in a 61-year-old patient [130].

A new magnetic therapy device built like a helmet housing a set of electromagnetic coils similar to a car's alternator has successfully been used on Parkinson's and Multiple Sclerosis patients to alieviate their symptoms and pain. [131]

Natural alternatives like this magnetic therapy helmet are creating new avenues to help Parkinson's, Alzheimer's and Multiple Sclerosis patients who can't be helped by drugs.

129. Sandyk, R.; *Magnetic Therapy Reverses Agraphia in a Parkinson's Patient,* International Journal of Neuroscience, No. 1996
130. George, M.S., et al; *Transcranial Magnetic Stimulation: A 21st Eentury Neurophychiatric Tool,* Journal of Neuropsychiatry, Fall 1996
131. Bardasanho, J., et al, Extra Cranial Helmet Treats Parkinson's and MS Patients, Magnetism in Biilogy and Medicine, Bologna, Italy, June 1997

SKIN DISEASE

CAUSE OF PARKINSON'S DISEASE
This disorder results from damage, of unknown origin, to the basal ganglia (nerve cell clusters in the brain). The difference between the healthy state and parkinson's disease is shown below.

Healthy state
during movement, signals pass from the brain's cortex, via reticular formation and spinal cord (pathway A), to muscles, which contract. Other signals pass, by pathway B, to the basal ganglia, these damp the signals in pathway A, reducing muscle tone so that movement is not jerky. dopamine, a nerve transmitter made in the basal ganglia, is needed for this damping effect. Another transmitter acetylcholine, inhibits the damping effect.

Parkinson's disease
In Parkinson's disease, degeneration of parts of the basal ganglia causes a lack of dopamine within this part of the brain. The basal ganglia are thus prevented from modifying the nerve pathways that control muscle contraction. As a result, the muscles are overly tense, causing tremor, joint rigidity, and slow movement. Most drug treatments increase the level of dopamine in the brain or oppose the action of acetylcholine.

Description
- The outermost covering of body tissue, which protects the internal organs from the environment. The skin is the largest organ in the body. Its cells are continually being replaced as they are lost by wear and tear.

The skin consists of a thin outer layer (the epidermis) and a thicker inner layer (the dermis). Beneath the dermis is the subcutaneous tissue, which contains fat. The *hair* and *nails* are extensions of the skin and are composed mainly of *keratin*, which is the main constituent of the outermost part of the epidermis.

The epidermis is made up of flat cells that resemble pacing stones when viewed under the microscope. Its thickness varies depending on the part of the body, being thickest on the soles and palms and very thin on the eyelids. It is generally thicker in men than in women and normally becomes thinner with age.

The outermost part of the epidermis is composed of dead cells, which form a tough, horny, protective coating. As these dead cells are worn away, they are replaced. The new cells are produced by rapidly dividing living cells in the innermost part of the epidermis. Between the outer and inner parts is a transitional region that consists of both living and dead cells.

Most of the cells in the epidermis are specialized to produce keratin, a hard protein substance that is the main constituent of the tough, outermost part of the epidermis. Some of the cells produce the protective pigment *melanin*, which determines skin color.

The dermis is composed of connective tissue interspersed with various specialized structures, such as hair follicles, *sweat glands*, and *sebaceous glands*, they produce an oily substance called *sebum*. The dermis also contains blood vessels, lymph vessels and nerves.

Parkinson's Disease Equal Opportunity Illness

Everyone has an opportunity to get Parkinson's if you live long enough. Every decade we live past 40 we lose 10% of our dopamine-producing brain cells. When you lose 805, you have Parkinson's, which is beyond most life spans. However, heavy drinking and drug use accelerate the dopamine loss. To protect yourself take Vitamins A, B. C & E, CoQ10, melatonin and DHEA, and you probably will never get it even if you are a heavy drinker.

The skin's most important function is to protect. It acts as the main barrier between the environment and the internal organs of the body, shielding them from injury, the harmful rays of sunlight, and invasion from infective agents, such as bacteria.

The skin is a sensory organ containing many cells that are sensitive to touch, temperature, pain, pressure, and itching. It also plays a role in keeping body temperature constant. When the body is hot, the sweat glands produce perspiration (which cools the body) and the blood vessels in the dermis dilate to dissipate the heat; if the body gets cold, the blood vessels in the skin constrict, which conserves the body's heat.

The epidermis contains a unique fatty substance that makes the skin waterproof - thus making it possible to set in a bath without soaking up the water like a sponge. The outer epidermis also has an effective water-holding capacity, which contributes to its elasticity and serves to maintain the body's balance of fluid and electrolytes. If the water content drops below a certain level, the skin becomes cracked, reducing its efficiency as a barrier.

Causes - Inflammation of the skin, sometimes due to an allergy, but in many cases occurring without any known cause. Many types of dermatitis are better known as *eczema* (for example, atopic, discoid, infantile, and hand eczema).

Apart from eczemas, the three main forms of skin inflammation are seborrheic dermatitis, contact dermatitis, and photodermatitis.

Seborrheic Dermatitis - this is a red, scaly itchy rash that develops on the face (particularly the nose and eyebrows), scalp, chest, and back. On the scalp it is the most common cause of *dandruff*. The rash often develops during times of stress, but its exact cause is unknown, Generally, the treatment of dermatitis must be tailored to each case. Applying topical corticosteroids and/or antimicrobials is often helpful. Also, gentle handling of the involved skin is imperative (i.e., avoidance of scratching and irritating substances - like detergents).

Contact Dermatitis - In this type, the rash is a reaction to some substance that comes in contact with the skin. The reaction may result from a direct toxic effect of the substance or may be an allergic response.

Among the more common causes of the reaction are detergents (including traces left in washed clothes), nickel (in watch straps, bracelets, necklaces, and the fastenings of underclothes), chemicals in rubber gloves and condoms, certain cosmetics, plants (such as poison ivy), and medications (among them the antibiotic neomycin in cream or droplet form).

The type of rash varies considerably according to the substance causing it, but it is often itchy, and may flake or blister; its distribution corresponds to the skin area in contact with the causative substance.

When it is not clear what substance is responsible, suspected chemicals are placed in contact with the skin of the back and are kept in place there with tapes for a few days to see whether any produces a patch of dermatitis. Once the offending substance is identified, it can then be avoided, if possible. A corticosteroid medication may be used for the treatment of an existing rash.

Herpes zoster - the medical term for shingles. Herpes zoster is an infection of the nerves that supply certain areas of the skin. It causes a painful rash of small, crusting blisters. After the rash heals, pain may persist for months or, rarely, years.

**Bet You Didn't Know
Your Skin is the Largest
Organ of the Human Body**
Your skin is the largest organ of the human body. Humans are hairier than chimps, but our hair is much shorter and generally lighter. Caucasians are the hairiest of the three races. All humans are the same species, skin color is an adaptation to climate. Caucasians, the last to develop, who got the worst real estate, are white because they blend with snow (handy when a sabre-toothed tiger is around) and white skin metabolizes vitamin D better and the least likely to frost bite. Yellow people developed the epicanthic fold (slant eyes) because they developed in windy, desert areas, Black skin protects against solar caused cancer, most whites on the Equator usually get skin cancer. If you took a Swede and put him in Africa, and an African in Sweden, in ten generations they'd completely change color.

Types - Herpes zoster often affects a strip of skin over the ribs on one side or, less commonly, a strip on one side of the neck and arm or the lower part of the body. Sometimes it involves the upper half of the face on one side; in this case, the eye may also be affected. Shingles in this area is known as herpes zoster ophthalmicus.

Herpes zoster is caused by the varicella-zoster virus, which also causes *chickenpox*. During an attack of chickenpox, most of the viral organisms are destroyed, but some survive and lie dormant in certain sensory nerves, remaining there for many years. In some people, a decline in the efficiency of the *immune system* (the body's defenses against infection) allows the viruses to reemerge and cause shingles.

The competence of the immune system declines with age; this decline is probably accelerated by stress and by the use of *corticosteroid drugs*. Herpes zoster commonly follows a stressful episode.

SHINGLES

The Herpes Zoster virus is everywhere. Stress seems to trigger an outbreak. One out of every 5 Americans will get it in their lifetime and it makes no difference to gender, race, location or time of year. As you age, years of stress take their toll; thus, 70% of the cases are of people over 70. If you live to 80, you have a 50-50 chance of having shingles.

Incidence - Herpes zoster is a common disease. Every year in the US, a few hundred people per 100,000 suffer an attack. It mainly affects people over 50 and the incidence rises with age. Herpes zoster is very common in people whose immune systems have been weakened either by diseases such as *lymphoma* or *Hodgkin's disease* or by treatment with *immunosuppressant* or *anticancer drugs*.

139

Symptoms and signs - the first indication is excessive sensitivity in the area of skin to be affected; this is soon followed by pain, which is sometimes severe and which may, until the rash appears, be mistaken for pleurisy or appendicitis.

After about five days, the rash appears, starting as small, slightly raised red spots that quickly turn to tense blisters, teeming with viruses. Within three days the blisters have turned yellowish and soon dry, flatten and crust over. During the next two weeks or so the crust drop off, often leaving small pitted scars.

The most serious feature of herpes zoster is pain following the attack. The pain is consequence of damage to the nerves, causing strong nerve impulses to be constantly produced and passed upward to the brain. The pain, which affects about one third of sufferers, may be severe and may last for months or years. The older the patient and the more pronounced the rash, the more likely the pain will be severe and persistent.

Sunburn Causes Cancer

FUN FACT EM RAYS
The Sun gives off two types of heating rays: ultraviolet and infrared. However, if you are sitting behind a pane of glass you will not tan because ultraviolet is blocked by glass.
Science
Encyclopedia

Skin Cancer - A malignant tumor in the skin. Skin cancer is one of the most common forms of cancer.

Basal cell carcinoma, squamous cell carcinoma, and malignant melanoma are common forms of skin cancer related to long-term exposure to sunlight. *Bowen's disease*, a rare skin disorder that can become cancerous, also may be related to sunlight exposure.

Less common types of skin cancer include *Paget's disease of the nipple* and *mycosis fungoides*; both produce inflammation similar to that of eczema. *Kaposi's sarcoma* is a type of skin cancer commonly found in patients with AIDS (although elderly patients may have Kaposi's sarcoma and not have AIDS).

Even though most skin cancers can be easily cured if treated early, many people die because they delay seeking treatment, especially from squamous cell carcinoma and malignant melanoma. Changes or new growths should be reported to a physician.

Symptoms - When you go to medical school, the professor teaching diagnostic procedures brings everything into sharp focus by breaking down a very complicated topic like *diagnosing a disease* to four simple Latin words which cover every possible human condition for sickness. These are: Calor (heat), Dolor (pain), Rubior (rash) and Tumor (lump). These four conditions (single or in combinations) represent everything that can go wrong with the human frame. Skin diseases have all four.

Magnetic Therapy - Magnet power for beautiful skin has successfully been used since Queen Cleopatra used magnetic jewelry to preserve her famous beauty. In studies of ancient pyramid tombs, magnets have been found with the pharaohs for their health in the next world. Hieroglyphics tell us that Cleopatra wore a magnetized tiara. This would stimulate the pituitary gland which would normally direct the skin to secrete more oil giving her a better suntan and more melanin for deeper, brighter skin. [132]

The famous study on skin recovery after plastic surgery was conducted by Dr. Daniel Man of the Surgery and Laser Center in Boca Raton, Florida. By using magnetic therapy there was a notable reduction in post-operative pain and much less bruising and inflammation of the skin. There was a marked acceleration of healing, most patients showed a 50% faster recuperative time. Also, most of his patients are wealthy matrons and business executives, plus aspiring actresses and models who appreciate the magnet's healing powers with scar tissue. [133]

Magnetic therapy works on the skin by optimizing cellular oxygen flow to the damaged skin which reduces swelling, inflammation, pain and protects against infections. This natural health alternative is the way to go when you have a skin problem.

132. Lawrence, Ron, et al, *Magnet Therapy, The Pain Cure Alternative*, Prima Publishing, Rocklin, CA, 1998.
133. Man, D., *Magnetic Therapy Influence on Wound Healing*, Journal of Plastic and Reconstructive Surgery, Dec. 1999

SPRAINS & TENDONITIS

Description - Tearing or stretching of the ligaments that hold together the bone ends in a joint, caused by a sudden pull. The fibrous capsule that encloses the joint may also be damaged. The most commonly sprained joint is the ankle; it is usually sprained as a result of 'going over" the outside of the foot so that the complete weight of the body is placed on the ankle.

A sprain causes painful swelling of the joint, which cannot be moved without increasing the pain. There may also be spasm (involuntary contraction) of surrounding muscles.

Causes - Over working your body.

Symptoms - Swelling, inflammation, pain, stiffness and soreness.

Magnetic Therapy - Magnets were proven effective by Dr. Linus Pauling in his ground breaking work on an increase of up to 300% cellular oxidation for which he won the 1954 Nobel Prize. This increase of oxygen to the inflammation area of a sprain and resultant tendonitis help remedy the situation faster with less stiffness, soreness and chronic pain. [134] The increased blood circulation caused by magnet's effect on the iron-rich hemoglobin in the oxygen carrying red blood cells helps dramatically in the acceleration of the healing process. [135] Magnets

134. de la Warr, G.W., *Biomagnetism*, Oxford Press, Oxford, England, 1967
135. Davis, Albert Roy; *Anatomy of Biomagnetics*, Litolibros Inc., San Lorenzo, Puerto Rico, 1974

were found to be very effective in healing the soft-fission lesions caused by a sprain and tendonitis. [136] Magnetic therapy was found very effective in a painful low back sprain from falling off a horse in a race competition. [137]

Magnetic therapy is the natural alternative for all types of sports or everyday sprains and tendonitis.

136. Coats, G.C., *Magnetic Therapy of Soft-Tissue Injury*, British Journal of Sports Medicine. UK, 1989
137. Salzberg, C.A., et al; *The Effects of Magnetism on a Spinal Cord Injured Patient*, Ostomy Wound Manage, 1995

Stomach Problems

Description - A hollow, saclike organ of the digestive system that is connected to the esophagus and the duodenum (the first part of the small intestine). The stomach lies in the left side of the abdomen under the diaphragm.

The stomach is flexible, allowing it to expand when food is eaten; in an adult, the average capacity is about 3 pints (1.5 liters). The stomach wall consists of layers of longitudinal and circular muscle, lined by special glandular cells that secret gastric juice, and supplied by blood vessels and nerves. A strong muscle at the lower end of the stomach forms a ring called the pyloric sphincter that can close the outlet leading to the duodenum.

Although the main function of the stomach is to continue the breakdown of food that is started in the mouth and completed in the small intestine, it also acts as a storage organ enabling food to be eaten only two or three times a day. Food would have to be eaten every 20 minutes or so if storage were not possible.

The sight and smell of food and the arrival of food in the stomach stimulate gastric secretion. The gastric juice secreted from the stomach lining contains pepsin (an enzyme that breaks down protein), hydrochloric acid (which kills bacteria taken in with the food and which creates the most suitable environment for the pepsin to work in), and intrinsic factor (which is essential for the absorption of vitamin B_{12} in the small intestine). The stomach lining also contains glands that secrete mucus which helps provide a barrier to prevent the stomach from digesting itself.

The layers of muscle produce rhythmic contractions about every 20 seconds that churn the food and gastric juice; the combined effect of this movement and the action of the digestive juice convert the semisolid food into a creamy fluid. This process takes varying lengths of time, depending on the nature of the food. Generally, however the richer the meal, the longer it takes to be emptied from the stomach. The partially digested food is squirted into the duodenum at regular intervals by the contractions of the stomach and relaxation of the pyloric sphincter.

Causes - Most stomach problems are a result of stress and/or poor nutrition/diet resulting in ulcers and cancer.

Symptoms - Loss of appetite, weight loss, bloating, nausea and vomiting.

Magnetic Therapy - Gastrointestinal problems, such as constipation and diarrhea tend to normalize when you drink magnetized water.

Although there has been little research into the health benefits of drinking magnetized water, anecdotal evidence shows that it has important benefits for general well-being, and also in treating some common condition and ailments.

Exposing water to a magnetic field arranges the water molecules in a more precise order. When this water is drank, it is believed that the ordering of the molecules makes it easier for the body's cells to ingest nutrients through the body tissues' water-based bathing fluids, and to expel waste products more efficiently, thus the cells have more energy for the body to use where it is needed.[138]

The Price of Ignoring Your Body's Warnings

If you only feel the pain of tendinitis during or after exercise, and it isn't too bad, you may be thinking that you could run a race or swim laps with that same amount of pain - if you had to. Or maybe you already have. In either case, you would be wise to realign your thinking. "You shouldn't play through pain unless your physician or physical therapist tells you otherwise." says American Physical Therapy Association's Bob Mangine. If pain is severe and you continue to abuse the tendon, it may rupture, says athletics trainer Bob Reese. And that could mean a long layoff, surgery, or even permanent disability. In other words, exercising through tendon pain today could mean staying on the sidelines for the remainder of your tomorrows.

Magnetized water helps stomach digestion because its aligned properties facilitates the breakdown of food into its component nutrients in the stomach; whereas, when it flushes into the colon it takes less energy and a greater proportion is absorbed. Thus you get better efficiency from your food intake according to Dr. H.L. Bansal of Johns Hopkins University School of Medicine, Baltimore, Maryland.[139]

In children suffering from chronic gastro-duodenitis, magnetic therapy was used to improve motor function of the stomach and reduce dyspepsia and pain which accompanies this stomach disorder.[140]

138. Coghill, Roger, *The Book of Magnetic Healing*, Simon and Schuster, London, UK, 2000
139. Bansal, R.S. and H.L.; *Magneto Therapy, Self-Help Book*, J. Bain Publishers Ltd., New Delhi, India, 1989
140. Petrokhina, L.M., et al; *Magnetic Therapy Used on Children Suffering from Strong Gastrodusdenitis*, Vopr Kurortol Fizioter Lech Fiz Kult, 1987

In another study of patients suffering from gastritis which caused gastroesophageal and duodeno-gastral reflexes (where stomach acid gushes up the esophagus giving a painful burning sensation). Of the 77 patients using magnetic therapy, 72% reported an easing of their condition. [141]

Magnetic therapy is a natural alternative for people who are tired of swallowing handfuls of antiacid pills (which incidently cause kidney and bladder stones). With this efficient method there are no side effects and it is 100% safe to use.

141. Bukanovich, O.s., et al, *Magnetotherapy Reduces Acid Refluxes,* Vopr Kurortaol Fizioter Lech Fiz Kult, 1996

TUBERCULOSIS

Description - An infectious disease, commonly called TB, caused in humans by the bacterium *MYCO-BACTERIUM TUBERCULOSIS*. Tuberculosis was once common worldwide and was a major killer in childhood and early adult life. In Europe, it was responsible for about one quarter of the deaths in the middle 19th century. Its incidence has fallen and continues to fall in developed countries, but tuberculosis remains a major problem in poorer countries.

DID YOU KNOW?
Up until 1920's stomach cancer was the #1 cancer in America. Now it is behind lung, colon, prostate, skin, pancreas, ovarian and brain. Why has it fallen to number 8? Because of refrigeration. the primary cause for stomach cancer is eating salted, pickled and smoked foods, especially, meat products. Also, refrigeration keeps our food much fresher. Thank you for the ice box.

Causes - infection is passed from person to person in airborne droplets (produced by coughing or sneezing). The bacteria breathed into the lungs then multiply to form an infected "focus." In a high proportion of cases the body's immune system then checks the infection and healing occurs, leaving a scar.

In about 5% of cases, however, the primary infection does not resolve. Spread occurs via the vessels of the lymphatic system to the lymph nodes. Sometimes at this stage bacteria enters the bloodstream and spread to other parts of the body; this is called miliary tuberculosis and may occasionally be fatal. In some people, the bacteria goes into a dormant state in the lungs and other organs only to become reactivated many years later. Progressive damage may then occur (e.g., cavities in the lungs).

In some cases, tuberculosis does not primarily affect the lung but may involve the lymph nodes (particularly of the neck), or the intestines, bones, or other organs. Such infections were especially common in bovine tuberculosis, acquired from contaminated cows' milk; this method of transmission has virtually disappeared from developed countries.

The incidence of tuberculosis in the US is about 8 to 10 new cases per 100,000 population annually and is falling. However, this still represents more than 20,000 new cases in the US per year. The incidence is much higher in certain racial or social groups, such as Hispanics, Haitians, and immigrants from Southeast Asia. The disease is also more common in deprived city areas, in the elderly, in patients with *immunodeficiency* disorders, in diabetics, alcoholics, and in people who are in close contact with a person with tuberculosis.

HEALTHY TIP

Do not drink iced drinks with your meal. First, you dilute the gastric acid making it less efficient in digestion, and secondly, hydrochloric acid will not be secreted if the stomach's internal temperature drops below 95° which only takes a few ice cubes. Then undigested food will move into your colon where it becomes a problem.

Worldwide, there are 30 million people with active tuberculosis; about 3 million die of the disease annually. Tuberculosis is most prevalent where resistance has been lowered by malnutrition and other diseases.

In the US, two types of preventive measures are used against tuberculosis. First is the use of *BCG vaccination* in high-risk groups. Second is *contact tracing*. Relatives and close friends of a tuberculosis victim are examined, X-rayed, and given a skin test so that tuberculosis is detected at an early state and the risk of spread to other people is reduced. Any person - especially a child - who has contact in a household with someone who has active tuberculosis is given an antituberculosis antibiotic drug as a preventative measure.

Symptoms - Because tuberculosis usually affects the lungs, the main symptoms include coughing (sometimes bringing up blood), chest pain, shortness of breath, fever and sweating (especially at night), poor appetite, and weight loss. The main complications of tuberculosis of the lungs are *pleural effusion* (collection of fluid between the lung and chest wall), *pneumothorax* (air between the lungs and chest wall) and, in some cases, progression of the disease to death.

Magnetic Therapy - Russia is currently drowning in a sea of MRD tuberculosis. Thousands are dying there because very little can be done. They are experimenting with magnets because pharmaceutical drugs have failed them in their battle against MRD-TB.

Dr. Khomenko led a team of Russian physicians in using strong magnets on the chest of patients suffering from pulmonary tuberculosis. [142] Another Russian doctor team, Dr. T.V. Kalinina and Dr. V.C. Churaev administered high frequency magnetic energy (similar to the 20,000 gauss MRI) on tuberculosis patients. They exhibited a 72% improvement rate in their TB conditions. [143]

142. Khominko, A., et al, Electro-magnetic Radiation in Comples Therapy for Pulmonary Tuberculosis, Millimetrovie Volni v Biologi I Mediccine, 1994.
143. Kalinina, T.V. and Choreav, V.D., High Energy MagnetismUsed at the Ryasan Regional TB Clinic, Mill. Vol. v Bio I Med., 1994

Dr. A.S. Solovena used magnetic therapy in conjunction with chemotherapy drugs (usually used for cancer patients). The patients he was dealing with were terminal MDR-TB and expected to die soon. It was a minor miracle but a third of them survived. [144]

It is amazing that magnetic therapy as a natural health alternative could have such miraculous results on such a deadly killer as MDR-TB.

144. Solov'ena, A.S., et al, *Magnetic Therapy and Chemotherapy Used on Patients with Advanced Pulmonary TB*, Probl Tuberk, 1987

Urinary Disease

Description - The part of the body concerned with the formation and excretion of urine. The urinary tract consists of the *kidneys* (with their blood and nerve supplies), the renal pelves (funnel-shaped ducts that channel urine from the kidneys into the ureters), *the ureters, bladder* and *urethra.*

The kidneys make urine by filtering blood. The urine collects in the renal pelves and then passes down the ureters into the bladder by gravity and peristalsis (wavelike contractions of the ureteric walls). Urine is then stored in the bladder until a sufficient amount is present to stimulate micturition (passage of urine). When the bladder contracts, the urine is expelled from the body via the urethra.

Causes - An infection anywhere in the urinary tract. *Urethritis* (inflammation of the urethra) may be caused by mechanisms other than infection, but cystitis (inflammation of the bladder) and *pyelonephritis* (inflammation of the kidneys) are nearly always caused by bacterial infection.

When urethritis is due to infection, the cause is usually a sexually transmitted disease, such as *gonorrhea* or

TB on the Rise

In America from 1940 to 1990, we've had a 50 year decline in TB cases. By 1990, we were ready to declare that TB had gone the way of yellow fever, leprosy and polio. However, TB became resistant to the two main drugs, isoniazid and rifampicin and some are multi-drug resistant (MOR). These two new strains are rising here, but worldwide we are in an MDR epidemic; especially, in the former Soviet Republics. There are now 50 million people who are dying with no hope of MRD-TB. The world is in trouble.

153

nonspecific urethritis, often caused by chlamydia organisms. Otherwise, urinary tract infection is usually caused by organisms that have spread from the rectum, via the urethra, to the bladder or kidneys. Infections can also be bloodborne.

Because of the shortness of the urethra in women, infections above the urethra are more common in women than in men. In many women, they occur without any identifiable underlying cause. In most men and some women, however, there is an identifiable cause, usually some factor that impairs the drainage of urine. In men, this may be an enlarged prostate gland *(see Prostate, enlarged)* or a *urethral stricture.*

Cranberry Juice to the Rescue
E.coli bacteria, usually found in the intestines, causes urinary infections. Cranberry juice has two compounds which flush these bacteria out of the urinary ducts and stops the infections.
New England Journal of Medicine

In either sex, urinary tract infection may be caused by a urinary tract *calculus* (stone), a *bladder tumor*, or a congenital abnormality of the urinary tract, such as a double kidney on one side. Defective bladder emptying as a result of *spina bifida* or spinal cord injury *(see Spinal injury)* leads almost inevitably to urinary tract infection. Urinary tract infection is also more common during pregnancy.

The risks of a urinary tract infection can be reduced by careful personal hygiene, drinking plenty of fluids, and regular emptying of the bladder.

Symptoms - Urethritis causes a burning sensation when passing urine. Cystitis causes a frequent urge to pass urine, lower abdominal pain, *hematuria* (blood in the urine), and often general malaise with a mild fever. An infection in the kidneys leads to pain in the loins and high fever.

Urethritis can lead to scarring of the urethra and formation of a urethral stricture. Cystitis, provided there is no upward spread to the kidneys,

Louis Pasteur — 1822-1895
This famous French microbiologist accomplished much during his life. His most famous claim to fame was his development of the Germ Theory of Disease in 1881. This cornerstone theory led to the establishment of the huge pharmaceutical industry which dominates the world of Medicine. He is also famous for pasteurization, the cure for rabies and the discoverer of the spores which cause tuberculosis.

Science Encyclopedia

does not usually produce complications. Without proper treatment, kidney infection can lead to permanent kidney damage, *septicemia* (spread of infective organisms to the blood), and *septic shock*. If a calculus in a kidney is the underlying cause of infection, it may grow rapidly during the course of the infection.

Magnetic Therapy - magnetized water is an excellent way to keep your urinary tract free from infections. It also improves digestion, reduces gastric acid, flatulence, acts as a diuretic, dissolves kidney/gall stones and has tremendous cleansing effects on the urinary system. [145]

Urinary problems release extra uric acid into the blood stream which crystalize and cause blockages; especially in gout. By maintaining proper urinary health through the use of magnetized water, you diuretically lower uric

145. Donnet, Louis; *Les Aimants pour votre Sante (Magnets for your Health)*, Editions Dangles, St-Jean-de-Braye, France, 1996

acid in the cariovascular system and help to lower the possibility of gout. [146]

Magnetic therapy is used successfully to reduce urinary inflammations. [147] Magnetic energy is also proven effective in patients suffering from urolithiasis (stone formation). [148]

The natural alternative use of magnetic energy is very important to keep your personal plumbing in tip-top, working shape.

Urinary Tract Infections

UTI's are not uncommon, especially in women. About 20% of all women suffer from at least one UTR in their life. **Women are more prone** to suffer from UTIs because the female urethra (the tube connecting your urinary bladder to the outside of your body) is only about an inch long. That's a short distance for bacteria to have to travel, so any bacteria that might be present near the urethral opening can easily infect the bladder. Men, on the other hand, have a long urethra, and they have significantly fewer urinary tract infections because the bacteria never make it up the urethra to the bladder.

146. Coghill, Roger, *The Book of Magnet Healing*, Simon and Schuster, London, UK, 2000
147. Stiller, M.J., et al, *Magnetic Therapy Used to Enhance the Reduction of Urinary Inflammation*, British Journal of Dermatology, 1992
148. Karczewska, M.; *Magnetolaser Therapy in the Treatment of Patients with Urolithiasis*, Med. Pr, 1996

CHAPTER IV

Summary

Christopher Columbus was told not to sail off into the western seas because everybody knows that the Earth is flat and you will fall off. Thomas Edison was told by his learned friends that you can't get light from an electric wire because there's nothing to burn. Albert Einstein's professor told him that he would never find any energy from a little atom. Carl Sagan was told to forget about space travel because everybody knows nothing can move in a vacuum . . . and perhaps you might be told there is no healing power from magnetic therapy.

Skepticism

- *It will never work*
- *It may work, but only with a little luck.*
- *I knew it would work.*
- *I thought of it first.*
    Anonymous

Well, I guess everybody's entitled to their opinion. After all it's a free country, right! Your family, friends and neighbors will all offer their advice. Just remember, it's always easier for them to deride a product because they can then always have the delicious moment of "I told you so!" Also, their "friendly" warning allows them to escape any responsibility of endorsing something they really don't know anything about.

This book you have just read gives you the answers to these critics and skeptics. You have just read the facts. Contrary to what some may say, there is a vast amount of scientific research that supports the benefits of magnetic therapy. This book is loaded with confirmation of magnetic therapy's ability to heal.

Let us look again at what we know about magnetic therapy facts. Magnetism is part of the eletromagnetic energy field that controls everything in the Universe. It is the force that holds *everything* God created together. From the planets revolving around the Sun, to the electrons revolving around a tiny atom; all are held in place by magnetism. Magnetism is what causes the flow of electrons from the negative pole to the positive. This is what creates electricity. You can never have electricity without magnetism, they go together like salt & pepper. Magnetism is what enables your brain to flow. Without the magnetic energy running through your body, you would cease to exist.

This primeval creative force is the cosmic glue that holds together the Universe and controls the evolution of humanity from your birth. This electromagnetic energy is the architect of the human body and governs your every bodily function in a perpetual electromagnetic interaction which occurs among your trillions of

HISTORICAL ADVANCE OF MODERN MEDICINE

2000 B.C. - Here take this root, it will cure you

500 A.D. - Don't take this root, digest this powder

1000 A.D. - Don't take this powder, drink this potion

1850 A.D. - Don't take this potion, swallow this pill.

1950 A.D. - Don't take this pill, take this antibiotic

2000 A.D. - Don't take this antibotic, chew on this root
It will cure you!
George McDermott, PhD.
Millennium Age

158

body cells.

The source of the electric energy that powers your body is from the flow of blood through your blood stream (cardiovascular system). Similar to our use of hydroelectric power, the water flowing thru a turbine creating electricity is like your blood flowing thru your arteries. The friction of the passing liquid creates an electromagnetic charge. In your body, this 85 watt charge powers your brain to think, your heart to pump and your limbs to move. Death occurs when the flow of magnetic energy stops. Your health, wellness and longevity are in direct correlation to the even production and distribution of this God-given energy.

After 40, your electromagnetic energy slows down and distribution becomes less regular. Your memory often momentarily fails and you jokingly refer to this as a "Senior Moment," when interrupted by stress, inflammation or artherioscelorsis. These blockages are signs that your body is deteriorating through disease, lack of exercise or most commonly, poor nutrition. You need to pay attention to these symptoms, for your body is crying out for your help. There are many things you can do to postpone and ease these aging problems.

Magnetic Therapy is one of the easy, inexpensive methods you can learn to use to naturally help your body maintain peak efficiency. There are 7 ways that Magnetic Therapy can assist your holistic rejuvenation.

1.   In 1954, Dr. Linus C. Pauling received the Nobel Prize for Chemistry for his theroy of valency. With this discovery, the magnetic properties of hemoglobin in blood became scientifically understood.. The 75% iron in blood transports oxygen throughout your body. Without this iron, you would suffocate. Many people; especially women, suffer from iron-deficiency  anemia, which makes you slow down because of lack of oxygen. Magnetic Therapy helps with greater oxidation and gives you more energy.

2. Dr. Pauling discovered that magnetized iron is not only a perfect carrier of energy but it also has a direct benefit of increasing the internal metabolism of the cell. Again, Magnetic Therapy helps with increased energy to alleviate chronic fatigue.

3. Magnetic Therapy, through negative ionization causes free flowing calcium ions to adhere to your skeleton. The FDA approves magnets for bone healing

4. Your body is over 70% of water. Magnetization causes the splitting of intermolecular bonds creating "wetter" water that flows easier. Therefore, Magnetic Therapy enables greater energy-producing circulation; plus, water molecules have easier passage into body cells. Again, this increases cellular energy, removes blockages and relieves pain in joints and muscles.

5. Your body is an excellent conductor of magnetic energy. This conductive property assists the trace mineral copper to defend against infections, builds red blood cells and relieves spasmodic conditions.

6. Before 1903, the U.S. Navy had to replace seawater intake pipes that cooled the engines every 5 years. But once they learned to magnetize the incoming seawater, the pipes no longer clogged because the sediment stayed in collodial suspension. Your body "pipes" work the same way. Magnetic Therapy helps reduce plaque build up which causes strokes and high blood pressure. **7.** When NASA first started its conquest of space, they found the astronauts were disoriented and uncoordinated upon a few revolutions around the Earth. They quickly discovered the cause was the beneficial magnetic influence here on Earth is absent in space. Therefore, they resolved the problem by including magnetism in their space suits which solved the problem.

With magnetic therapy products you truly do get what you pay for, not all are created equal. You need to be certain:
1. The strength in the magnets being used will serve your needs.
2. The product, whether slept on or strapped on is comfortable and easy to use.
3. Make sure that the quality of material used is designed for the specific application.
4. To look very closely at the overall workmanship, such as stitching, fit and finish, of the product.

"I have found only a choice few that meet the higher standards that I have listed." I have personally found that Benefit Health products and their Visco Medic Sleep system meets all of my criteria and has become my own personal preference (I sleep on it).

Everybody living on Earth past the age of 25 will benefit from a little magnetic therapy. It is non-invasive to your body and it gently heals you without your daily realization. Take advantage of this wonderful, all-natural treatment to better your life and health.

INDEX

A

B

E

F

G

H

I

M

N

O

P

R

S